In Performance

EDITED BY CAROL MARTIN

To perform is to imagine, represent, live and enact present circumstances, past events and future possibilities. Performance takes place across a very broad range of venues from city streets to the countryside, in theatres and in offices, on battlefields and in hospital operating rooms. The genres of performance are many, from the arts to the myriad performances of everyday life, from courtrooms to legislative chambers, from theatres to wars to circuses.

IN PERFORMANCE is devoted to national and global theatrical narratives of the twenty-first century. Written by both established and new playwrights, translated by accomplished translators, the series consists of plays and performance texts introduced by scholarly essays that provide the theatrical, cultural and political contexts for the work. This series is aimed at people who want to read diverse dramatic and performance literature to study the ways in which theatre is critiquing complex local and global political and theatre discourses, and, of course, for those who want to stage new works.

IN PERFORMANCE will include active scholarship, readable thought and engaged analysis across the broad spectrum of performance literature.

armEd reSPonse

PLAYS FROM SOUTH AFRICA

EDITED BY DAVID PEIMER

LONDON NEW YORK CALCUTTA

Seagull Books 2009

Relativity © Mpumelelo Paul Grootboom (paul@statetheatre.co.za)
Bush Tale © Martin Koboekae (martinkobo@gmail.com)
Hallelujah! © Xoli Norman (bluejazzcool@yahoo.com)
Reach © Lara Foot Newton (larafoot@telkomsa.net, footlara@gmail.com)
Armed Response © David Peimer (dpeimer@yahoo.com)

Note: Under international law, the rights for all plays are reserved and permission must be obtained from the individual writers. This can be done through applying to the writers or the editor at: dpeimer@yahoo.com

ISBN-13 (HB) 978 1 9064 9 708 8
ISBN-13 (PB) 978 1 9064 9 707 1

British Library Cataloguing-in-Publication Data

A catalogue record for this book is available from the British Library

Typeset by Seagull Books, Calcutta, India

Printed and bound in India by Rockwel Offset, Calcutta

CONTENTS

INTRODUCTION

DAVID PEIMER

HISTORICAL CONTEXT

Since 1994, South Africa has gone through a remarkable transformation; from 46 years of being a totalitarian state (1948–94) with legally institutionalized and enforced racism at every level of social, economic, geographic, and cultural life, to a democracy. When the cold war ended in 1989, the apartheid state started to collapse, but few expected a revolution to be negotiated in a mostly peaceful manner. This negotiation occurred from 1990 to 1994, and was widely called the "Negotiated Revolution." In 1994, Nelson Mandela was elected the country's first black president as the non-racial, democratic state was formed.

For nearly four years after 1996, The Truth and Reconciliation Commission helped entrench this mostly peaceful transition to democracy. In essence, if the perpetrators of murder or torture (the Death Squads, police, and army units) told the truth to the victims or their families in their presence, they were given amnesty. The victims (or their families) got truth, not justice nor revenge. Thousands of people's experiences were told in dusty halls all over the country and shown on TV most days. Often, the perpetrators had to also physically act out their methods of torture in front of their victims and the Commissioners in these halls. The country held its collective breath to see whether truth (and forgiveness) could triumph over vengeance and denial. In the words of Cynthia Ngwenyu, the mother of one of the murdered "Gugulethu Seven" speaking at the Truth and Reconciliation Commission: "This thing called reconciliation . . . If I am understanding it correctly . . . if it means this man who has killed my son, if it means he becomes human again, this man, so that I, so that all of us, get our humanity back . . . then I agree, then I support it."[1]

---

1 *Truth and Reconciliation Commission of South Africa Report*, VOL. 5, Chapter 2 (Cape Town: South African Government Publishers, 1998).

The Truth and Reconciliation Commission revealed the pain of generations who endured the brutality of the apartheid regime. Such a societal experience has little to do with reductive notions of a miraculously forgiving Rainbow Nation. Ordinary people (not the policy-makers or regime's rulers) gathered day after day in these bare community halls throughout the country, to face their perpetrators across a table as millions of South Africans watched on TV. The nation was gripped by the painful, but mysterious, power of truth and the glimpses of humanity it engendered. Most times, revealing the truth did not lead to an acquiescent sense of redemptive forgiveness, but, in a more profound way, aspired to help humanize a traumatized society.

It is now more than a decade since the Commission ended. As the experience of the "Negotiated Revolution" unfolds, new methods of capturing and conveying the subjective and societal revelations of truth, the discovery of the "Other," the collective and individual trauma are being explored by artists and theater-makers. Additional important themes include the complexities of new-found freedom and a sense of belonging. But there is no false euphoria: removing the claws of totalitarianism has also revealed feelings of abandonment, revenge, and anger. Since the late 1990s, fear, a disillusionment with certain ideals of the revolution, corruption, and extremely violent crime have also formed part of the South African experience. This all takes place in a country where one in nine persons has AIDS (most without treatment) and many live in abject poverty.

The complex and competing realities that make up South Africa today has resulted in an emerging sense of a dynamically changing, multifaceted South African identity that is deeply engaged with both past and present structures of power. These thematic interactions are reflected in the plays in this anthology.

THEATER IN POST-APARTHEID SOUTH AFRICA

The legacy of four decades of apartheid continues to deeply inform cultural, social, and political life in South Africa. However, wide-ranging, new forms of theater are being created to reflect these current themes. As the plays show, there is no single dominant aesthetic style, but, rather, a paradigm of evolving and eclectic forms.

During apartheid, a South African genre of protest theater emerged and included Black Consciousness theater (the work of Maishe Maponya, Matsamela Manaka and others) and, from a different perspective, theater created by whites in opposition to the racially determined privilege they inhabited. The plays were often scripted through the process of the workshop method. The making and staging of these plays created a fleeting, perhaps illusory but needed sense of "normal" collaboration among black and white actors (which was not allowed in most other forms of social, cultural, political, and geographic interaction—apartheid was segregation at every level of societal interaction, from toilets to beaches to bank entrances to places of work, living, and study, to many jobs being "for whites only," to the denial of the vote).

In order to directly confront apartheid, the theater of these times took the form of devised theater created in collaborative workshops. This often led to a stereotyping of character and simplicity of narrative with an attending binary of justice or injustice. Plays such as *Woza Albert!* (1981) by Mbongeni Ngema, Percy Mtwa, and Barney Simon and *The Island* (1973) by John Kani, Winston Ntshona, and Athol Fugard were able to transcend this stereotyping and its attending binary thinking about justice and injustice.

In *Woza Albert!* two actors portray a multitude of character types that are extremely varied yet do not drive the dramatic action of the play. Like the great satires of Gogol, Aristophanes, and others, character types are subservient to the key idea of the play. The structure of *Woza Albert!* avoids the binaries conventionally created by polemical characters in conflict with one another by making a question the premise of the play: What would happen to Jesus Christ if he came to apartheid South Africa? This question lifts the play into a profound and complex sense of drama resulting in a theater driven by a core dramatic action that is both uniquely universal and imaginative. *Woza Albert!* became the most popular play to ever come out of South Africa, and toured the world. Together with this sense of satire, the text calls for an extremely physical performance, song, dance, minimal use of set and props, and fantastical shifts in space and time (mostly evolved from the township-theater style of Gibson Kente, the great mentor of many black performers and writers).

Satire was, arguably, one of the most effective tools against the state and attracted the greatest audiences. *The Island* is another prime example. Set on Robben Island, off the Cape Town coast, (where Mandela and many others were imprisoned for decades) the two male actors create great humor as they play prisoners trying to stage Sophocles' *Antigone* in the prison. Much rough humor occurs as one prisoner does not want to dress as a woman for something called theater (he has barely ever seen a play), and his friend teases and urges him to do so. This may seem banal, but one can never forget that they are in prison because of their political belief in a non-racial society. Gradually, one stops laughing at the playful antics of a very masculine man trying to resist dressing up as a woman, and the full force of the play's meaning dawns on us. This force is heightened precisely because of the humor that has gone before.

Much protest theater was made on a shoestring budget, and, it can be argued, often lacked a subtle range of character and narrative, theatrical craft, complex grasp of questions of human existence, and frequently lapsed into limited and obvious binaries of race. The sentiment at the time was that art and theater needed to be a weapon against the state, given the abhorrence of living in the reality of a racial and dictatorial paradigm.

These pre-1994 forms still have a powerful influence on contemporary South African theater. Since the democratic elections, these have been greatly developed in radically new directions. In this anthology, one sees how these new forms have built on this tradition. The playwrights' vision of human existence has become ever-more complex and multilayered in the post-revolutionary society. The plays show a contemporary complexity which incorporates the legacy of protest theater and ideologically informed narratives and characters as a starting point for new theatrical forms.

This new theater has been achieved in a number of ways. Firstly, it embraces the writer rather than the workshop group as the central propagator of enquiry. The writers then investigate ways of building on the "township" tradition of employing song, dance, heightened physicality, satire, and leaps in space and time. This is done because they are interested in reflecting current radical societal changes. The result is that the plays combine the aesthetics of non-realism and realism, multidimensional characters and simple comedic caricature, crafted dramatic situations and narrative, and the visual pleasure of more abstract, imagistic design.

In both esthetics and subject matter, South African theater has evolved from the binaries of justice and injustice, and become a place where ideology and history profoundly inform, but do not dictate, the obsessive drive of human passions.

THE PLAYS

The plays I have included in this anthology reflect prevalent and emerging trends in both subject matter and esthetics in South Africa. Equally important is that they all interact with and problematize the post-apartheid historical moment. My aim is to reflect and identify significant trends which characterize contemporary South African theater. Therefore, this anthology does not include the range of community theater done in school halls, centers of religion, and community spaces that deals with the vast range of issues confronting South Africans, e.g. AIDS, poverty, unemployment, lack of education, dearth of sanitation, health care, housing and electricity, running water, voter and gender education. The anthology also omits strictly "traditional" African performance involving ritual, storytelling, song and dance which is often participatory and for a specific purpose such as initiation rites and ancestor worship. It is important to note this, since during apartheid this was restricted or done for tourism, whereas now it is seen as reaffirming a sense of social and historical identity. Also, these forms have influenced "township" and protest theater of the past, and find expression in contemporary theater.

Aspects of this moment are vividly captured in the play *Relativity: Township Stories* by Mpumelelo Paul Grootboom and Presley Chweneyagae which premiered in 2005. *Relativity: Township Stories* is about a serial killer on the loose in a township. The gritty, physicalized, harsh violence unleashed in the play is captured in a highly visual, postmodern cinematic style with a soundtrack to manipulate mood. Not by chance have the writers been called the "Township Tarantinos."

South Africa has a bloody history, and, since the late 1990s—post the Mandela and the Truth and Reconciliation Commission period—it has become one of the most violent, murderous countries on earth (20,000 murders a year, 40,000 rapes, 150,000 assaults, rampant car-jacking, robbery, bombing of bank ATMs—the list goes on).[2] "Life is hard, death is easy" is the phrase from the play that best expresses its central concern. With the murders, rapes, and beatings by poverty-stricken, township men with nothing to lose, lies a sense of an identity brutalized beyond humanity, revealed with sharp, dark humor. This is not the "rainbow nation" identity of Bishop Tutu's hopes, but is part of a very South African identity burnt into the soul by the extreme violence, racism, and poverty in its collective memory and current reality.

Freedom has brought a sense of belonging for some, but many remain marginalized from the partial spreading of wealth and access to the bare

---

2 "Crime Stats. A Wake-up Call for Government," *Mail and Guardian Newspaper* (Johannesburg), 3 July 2007.

essentials of life. This sense of abandonment—both current and historical—has sparked a deep anger, and this (together with corruption or lack of effective policing) can be linked to the extremely brutal violence which all South Africans experience. When it opened, the play was highly controversial as it critiques aspects of the new democratic state, but the writers have not flinched from revealing these harsh realities. They know township life extremely well, and Grootboom is a highly respected, award-winning author and director. Chweneyagae has recently starred in the Oscar-winning film *Tsotsi* (South African slang for criminal).

In an entirely different vein, *Bush Tale* by Martin Koboekae (premiered in 2006) has a subtle, gentle, and humorous style. The play poignantly depicts the mistrust prevalent when two people from extremely different cultural backgrounds meet by chance in a deeply rural part of South Africa. A white woman from a conservative background encounters a witty black man from a politicized one. She is trying to get away from her husband who is on holiday at a nudist colony. The black man is on his way to the mill where he works, and pushes a rickety wheelbarrow laden with bags of corn.

As the play evolves, the strange, isolated space of their meeting becomes a poetic image which lifts it out of naturalism. With much trepidation and distrust, they interact with each other. One can sense extremely subtle glimpses of the influence of the Truth and Reconciliation Commission. The characters try to confront their own personal and cultural memory of white privilege and black trauma as they attempt to discover the meaning of Otherness. This is done through a theatricalizing of the Truth and Reconciliation Commission's focus on revelations of "truth." The Commission had the aim of "humanizing" the sense of Otherness which was enforced by apartheid ideology. The play is not in any way a literal version of the Commission's approach or content but operates on the metaphysical level of "revealing truth" through a gentle encounter of two characters. But, deeper than this, one sees the play as a delicate and thoughtful moment in time during which these characters try, with great trepidation, wariness, humor, and curiosity to engage with prejudice, stereotype, history, and cultural memory.

This brief moment is captured in a landscape of stark, rural desolation. In this landscape, the characters find a few gentle and unpredictable stolen moments that enable them to partly see beyond the racially determined identities they have inherited. As we are drawn into their world, they struggle to face this truth and the internal changes these insights would demand. Exploring changes like this have been a profound part of the award-winning playwright and novelist Koboekae's life.

If *Bush Tale* captures the timeless feel of a fleeting encounter in which Otherness is gradually revealed, *Hallelujah!* depicts the violent and compassionate heart of contemporary township life.

Reading *Bush Tale* followed by *Hallelujah!* articulates the current South African experience—the country is a land of extreme contrasts: Third/First World, race and class divisions, violence and compassion, poverty and disease, and a land which has provided 30 percent of the world's gold. During apartheid, most other tensions were subjugated to the harsh racial paradigm but since freedom these tensions have unleashed a new multilayered dynamic sense of identity. *Bush Tale* expresses a hope, perhaps a dream whereas Xoli Norman's play *Hallelujah!* delves into the violent, poverty-racked reality of township life, relieved only by moments of rough township humor and music.

Like the other black writers in this anthology, Norman grew up in the tough townships of apartheid, managed to be one of very few young black people "permitted" to study at a "white" university, and went on to become very well-known as a playwright, composer, TV writer, and director. He has also taught at the formerly "white" University of the Witwatersrand, Johannesburg, where he had originally studied. Like others, he had to live in Soweto, travel for hours to study every day and read by candlelight as he was not allowed to live in the "white" areas close to the university. For *Hallelujah!* he was one of the first black playwrights to win the Schreiner South African Young Artist award in 2002.

Highly popular in South Africa, *Hallelujah!* (premiered in 2002) is the play "black audiences hate to love" as author Xoli Norman puts it.[3] The narrative is deceptively simple as it follows the ordinary lives of one black family. We experience them at home, and in a jazz club in the huge, sprawling township of Soweto (now part of Greater Johannesburg). But within this seemingly simple narrative of family life, love and generation conflict lies a vision of life full of vivid, extremely personal experiences forged in the death throes of apartheid. However, after this, many have come to feel abandoned by the new structures of power as their dreams and hopes have not be fulfilled (e.g. lack of delivery on poverty, running water, electricity, housing, sanitation, education, crime, unemployment, corruption).

---

3 Xoli Norman, Unpublished interview, Johannesburg, 2008.

The Truth and Reconciliation Commission's theme of trying to "human-ize" the brutality burning in the collective memory can be felt as the characters' humanity, wit, and compassion emerge to transcend the past. But the true power of the play occurs in a moment of great dramatic irony. Just as we are drawn into the warmth of their humanity, the characters fall prey to the mur-derous random violence engulfing the country. "I wanted to investigate the si-lences in the euphoria of this 'new' democracy," Norman said.[4]

Central to the play is the lively and haunting township jazz that is played live during most of the play. Paradoxically, as the subject matter draws one deeper into the daily fear of murder most South Africans live with, the music inspires one by incorporating traditional rural Xhosa music within an urban township sound. The blues and jazz sounds come from the memories of a pas-toral past and a distinct collective identity that counters the harsh landscape of Johannesburg and Soweto. The singing, and the evocative chanting, invests both the singer and the audience with a kind of hope, "a stubbornness to this harshness that mediates the brutal events in the play. As they struggle to nego-tiate the rough, post-apartheid landscape of the play, the audience and char-acters find solace and sanity in the landscape of a South African jazz."[5]

Living between the extremes of new freedom and fear, the characters live out their hopes and anxieties under the shadow of an extremely violent past and present. The play raises the possibility that perhaps even in this historical moment, idealistic euphoria will always contain the seeds of its murderous past.

It is this past which is subtly and emotionally confronted in Lara Foot New-ton's play *Reach* (premiered in Hanover, Germany, 2007). This is done ironically as the play is set in the future. As with Norman and the other writers in this an-thology, Foot Newton has devoted most of her life to creating new South African theater. She is one of the most important innovators in the country, constantly taking the workshop process into the realm of the writer, and has developed a distinct esthetic while never ceasing to question the role of theater in the cur-rent cultural and political paradigm. Because of this, and the quality of her work, she has received international recognition—the most recent being the International Rolex Arts Award (2004), which enabled her to be a protégé of Sir Peter Hall, and the Sundance Festival assisting with adapting her play, *Tshep-hang* (2003), into a film.

---

4 Ibid.

5 Ibid.

Like *Bush Tale*, *Reach* stages an encounter between two characters, one black and one white. *Reach* tells the story of an elderly white South African woman living in a rural part of South Africa, near a former "blacks only" township, and her hesitant, yet lively, relationship with a young black man who visits her. The play is set in the Eastern Cape in a remote, rural, unforgiving landscape conveying a sense of a heightened, distilled, poetic atmosphere and locating the play between the shifting worlds of realism and a haunting, surreal strangeness. It is located in a very concrete post-apartheid reality; yet, like a painting, it also feels like a moment in time lifted out of this reality and abstracted into a world of visual and emotional poetry.

This constant shift between a "real" and a surreal or imaginative theatrical experience represents a prevalent characteristic of many new South African plays—it is an esthetic which tries to grasp the nuances of an ever-changing, multifaceted paradigm of identities in this post-revolutionary era.

Reach's subject matter delicately problematizes a lawless South Africa lurching towards an uncertain future without the "rule of law." From the beginning we discover that Solomon has a terrible secret to tell Marion about her murdered son; when the secret is revealed at the end of the play, there is the suggestion of a possible unsentimental redemption, an elusive glimmer of what a South African future could be. But the play is not just about the revelation of buried historical secrets and the hope for redemption their revelation holds; it is about the experience of personal, cultural, and historical abandonment.

It is deeply ironic that, after the Truth and Reconciliation Commission, both hope and abandonment should emerge as prevalent South African themes. *Reach* does not describe this development; it gets inside the very nerve of the tension inherent in these conflicting feelings.

Getting inside this nerve is a key focus of *Armed Response*, by David Peimer and Martina Griller (premiered in 2006). As with the other writers in the anthology, Peimer has been committed to creating new South African theater, usually with the aim of challenging the status quo, whether it be the devastating effects of apartheid ideology or the current tensions revealed in this brief moment of democratic freedom.

Armed Response follows a young German photographer who arrives to do her first assignment in Johannesburg. Excited and free-spirited, she meets Vusi who works for the Armed Response private security company. Vusi is a streetwise Soweto township man whose friends are gangsters who also work for the company. As the photographer meets her neighbors, corrupt police, gangsters, certain strange and frightening experiences happen to her and she succumbs to the omnipresent fear of being murdered in liberated South Africa.

The play's deeper existential themes of freedom and fear within the new democracy are located within the specific political context of the implications of massive privatization of security in South Africa. Why do armed private security guards outnumber police five to one in a multi-billion business? What happens to ordinary people when policing is privatized? For these companies, no crime means no business, no profit. Crime does pay. What happens to the enticement of corruption when security is privatized? It is surely a seductive temptation for police to be bought off by this new, mass-scale business. From the earliest times of colonization, South Africa has always been a criminalized society. As Nobel prize winner J. M. Coetzee puts it: "The crime wave is . . . anything but new . . . Raiding . . . of early colonial times had a peculiar conceptual status . . . (today) . . . thousands get up each morning . . . set off on raids . . . raiding is their business . . . their occupation."[6]

Armed Response explores the nuances of what it means to live in a criminalized or "raiding" society, when, ironically or predictably, the official ideology espouses its opposite. What differentiates the play from being yet another piece about crime is the play's context—the privatization of security and its motive of profit. Within this context, we experience the characters as ordinary people caught in the nuanced dilemma of trying to deal with, and distinguish between, valid fear and creeping paranoia. What happens to individuals and a society when these latter two emotions are blurred? In the context of a recently liberated but barely policed society, how do freedom and fear work in the psyche of individuals and a society caught in the enticing grip of a security-driven business for profit? Living in a society where criminalization (or "raiding") is a "norm," the characters in the play grasp that Faustian bargains are the reality, and democratic ideals the dream. At a more universal level, the play suggests that when one lifts the veneer of sophisticated ideology (freedom, democracy), one discovers the myth of Faust as the central, enduring reality of human interaction.

Aesthetically, *Armed Response* is cinematic in form. As in *Relativity: Township Stories*, each scene is visually composed within the overall emerging image. *Armed Response* moves from the esthetics of realism into a haunting, surreal

---

6 J. M. Coetzee, *Diary of a Bad Year* (London: Random House, 2007), pp. 103–06.

dream-like world as Anna and Vusi become entwined in a web of events over which they have very little control. Anna is a photographer and the play evolves into a world where, like a photograph, a moment in time is lifted out of reality and framed in a world of visual and emotional poetry.

This anthology "photographs" a post-revolutionary society and reveals a remarkably fluid and dynamically changing sense of identity. Through the plays, South Africa's theatrical esthetic tradition and the radically new influences that characterize prevalent trends emerge. Presenting this brief moment in time and history on the stage invites the audience to see the collision of historical and contemporary forces contained in this moment.

Disillusioned with the betrayal of the ideals of the French Revolution, Georg Buchner wrote: "The individual is merely the foam on the wave of history."[7] In contrast, Nelson Mandela, in his inauguration address as President in 1994 said: "Our greatest fear is not that we are inadequate; our greatest fear is that we are powerful beyond measure."[8]

Ultimately, the writers in this anthology go to the root of this all too human dramatic conflict of ideas.

FURTHER READING

COPLAN, D. 1985. *In Township Tonight: South Africa's Black City Music and Theatre.* London: Longmans.

CROW, B. and C. Banfield. 1996. *An Introduction to Post-Colonial Theatre.* Cambridge: Cambridge University Press.

DAVIS, G. and A. Fuchs (eds). 1996. *Theatre and Change in South Africa.* Amsterdam: Harwood Academic Publishers.

ETHERTON, M. 1982. *The Development of African Drama.* London: Hutchinson.

HOFMEYER, I. 1993. *Oral Historical Narrative in a South African Chiefdom.* London: Heinemann.

KAVANAGH, R. 1985. *Theatre and Cultural Struggle in South Africa.* London: Zed Books.

KERR, D. 1995. *African Popular Theatre.* London: Heinemann.

---

7 Michael Patterson (ed.), *Buchner: The Complete Plays* (London: Methuen, 1987), p. 280.

8 Nelson Mandela, Inaugural Speech, Pretoria, May 1994.

MBITI, J. 1980. *African Religions and Philosophy*. London: Heinemann.

NDLOVU, D. (ed.). 1986. *Woza Afrika! An Anthology of South African Plays*. New York: George Braziller Inc.

ROSS, R. 1999. *A Concise History of South Africa*. Cambridge: Cambridge University Press.

SCHIPPER, M. 1982. *Theatre and Society in Africa*. Johannesburg: Ravan Press.

SOYINKA, W. 1995. *Myth, Literature and the African World*. Cambridge: Cambridge University Press.

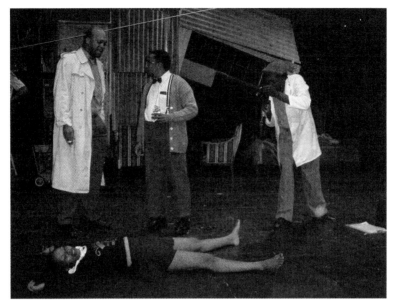

FROM LEFT TO RIGHT: *Pogiso Mogwera (Rocks), Tebogo Maboa (Molomo), Prince Sithole (Ranko), Patricia Mlambo (Bongi). Photograph by Mpumelelo Paul Grootboom.*

RELATIVITY: TOWNSHIP STORIES

MPUMELELO PAUL GROOTBOOM
AND PRESLEY CHWENEYAGAE

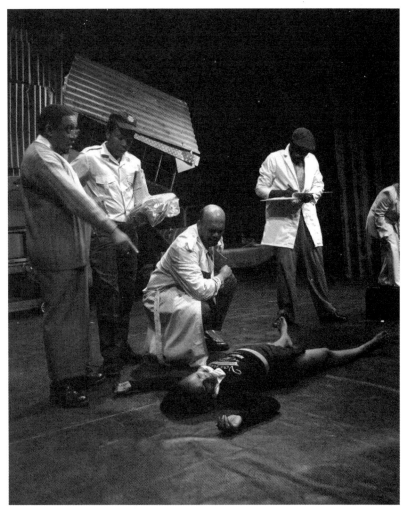

FROM LEFT TO RIGHT: *Tebogo Maboa (Molomo), Presley Chweneyagae (Policeman), Pogiso Mogwera (Rocks), Prince Sithole (Ranko), Patricia Mlambo (dead girl). Photograph by Mpumelelo Paul Grootboom.*

Relativity: *Township Stories* was developed through the State Theatre and premiered at the 2005 National Grahamstown Festival, South Africa, with the following cast:

BONGI	Patricia Mlambo
MOLOMO	Tebogo Maboa
ROCKS	Pogiso Mogwera
RANKO	Prince Sithole
SUZIE	Ntshepiseng Eunice Montshiwa
UNIFORM (POLICE OFFICER)	Presley Chweneyagae
DARIO	Karabo Kgokong
MATLAKALA	Refilwe Mokgotlhoa
DORAH	Ntshepiseng Eunice Montshiwa
DAN	Mahlubi Kraai
MAVARARA	Thabo Sekgobela
MAMIKI	Ntshepiseng Eunice Montshiwa
THABO	Zenzo Nqobe
THULI	Innocentia Manyaka
MIHLOTI	Kedibone Christina Tholo
MHLABA	Nyiko Prince Sithole
EXTRAS	Fumani Shilubana
	Presley Chweneyagae
DIRECTOR	Mpumelelo Paul Grootboom
	Presley Chweneyagae

ACT I

Prologue

Music. A piercing scream from a female voice comes from backstage. The girl, Bongi (18 years), comes on stage, running here and there, screaming for her dear life. She is panting; her clothing is torn . . . She takes a center spot on stage, still panting loudly but no longer screaming. She acts as if she is hiding behind something. A spotlight is on her and it is accentuating her fright . . . All of a sudden, she acts like the chaser has found her. The lights change again. Bongi runs round and round in large circles. The catching, the screaming, the raping and the killing follow. She is strangled with her G-string. Bongi is miming all this action—she is alone on stage, the killer invisible . . . Music fades off when she dies.

Beat 1

When the lights come up again, we have two or three uniformed cops standing over Bongi's dead body. The two of our story's detectives come through: one is very short (Det. Sgt James Molomo) and the other very tall (Det. Sgt Rocky Motshegare). The pathologist, Ranko, is already there.

ROCKS (*to a female uniformed cop*). Suzie!

SUZIE (*with a morning smile*). Hi, Rocks.

ROCKS. *O santse o rata banna?*[1]

SUZIE (*frowns*). Oho!

RANKO. Rocks.

ROCKS. Yes, Ranko, howzit?

RANKO. Molomo.

MOLOMO. Hey! (*They shake hands. Molomo kneels before the dead body.*) Does she have a name?

---

1 I see you still love men?

UNIFORM. We found no documents on her, no ID.

MOLOMO. Who called it in?

UNIFORM. Anonymous call.

RANKO. Looks like she was strangled with her underwear.

MOLOMO. A G-string?

RANKO. Yes. I think the strangler is back in action.

MOLOMO. I told you, Rocks, this is the third body now . . . I told you we have a serial killer on our hands.

ROCKS. We're not sure yet if it's the same arsehole. Let's investigate, gentlemen, and not make assumptions.

RANKO. But it's the same modus operandi, Rocks. Same signature.

UNIFORM (*showing them her sandals and a piece of clothing*). We found these on the other side of the bush . . .

ROCKS. What're these?

UNIFORM. Sandals and a top. Looks like she was being chased around before she was killed.

ROCKS. Is that your opinion?

UNIFORM. Yes, sir.

ROCKS. Look here, Constable, if I want your opinion I'll ask for it . . . but, until you pass your detective exam, keep it to yourself.

MOLOMO. But he's right, Rocks—and, if that's the case, then it's definitely the G-string Strangler.

ROCKS. G-string Strangler? You still call him that?

MOLOMO. What?

ROCKS. Do you want us to write reports and investigate a killer, naming him after women's underwear?

MOLOMO. Give him a name then.

ROCKS. You see, Mouth, just be—

MOLOMO. Don't call me Mouth!

ROCKS. Just because you have a bad name doesn't mean you have to make up for that by giving these killers pathetic names.

MOLOMO. You're out of line, Rocks, I don't have a bad name!

ROCKS. Your surname is a body part! How is that not a bad name?

MOLOMO (*getting angry*). *Wa itse keng* Rocks, *re tlo gogana ka dihempe* if you go on *ka matlhapa a*.[2]

RANKO. You're out of line, Rocks. My name is also a body part.

Ranko and Molomo improvise their protests against Rocks and Rocks interrupts/overlaps them saying—

ROCKS. Hey, hey, hey, look here, gentlemen, it's not my fault . . . I'm not the one who gave you your names. Let's get back to work, please! (*Kneels at the body*) So . . . "Ranko" . . . When was she killed?

RANKO. It's hard to say, but . . . I'd say not over twenty-four hours . . .

ROCKS. Was she also raped, like the last one?

RANKO. Yes, she's got semen all over her pubic area . . . and she's bruised all over.

Rocks picks up the G-string on her neck and moves off, smelling it.

ROCKS. We really must catch this bastard before he becomes a national celebrity.

Soft music. The two detectives begin to address the audience. The dead body is not cleared but is kept on stage for reference later in the interrogation room.

MOLOMO. The girl actually turned out to be one Sibongile Mabaso . . .

ROCKS. And with further investigation and with the help of the community, we were able to establish that she was one of those loose girls of the township— one of her neighbors even went to the extent of calling her "a weekend special."

MOLOMO. In short, we established that she was no stranger of the night—a regular at many of the roughest *shebeens*[3] of the township . . . She is said to have been loud, rude, and quite an extrovert.

---

2 You know what, Rocks, we're going to fight if you go on insulting me like this.

3 An illicit bar or club where excisable alcoholic beverages are sold without a licence. In South Africa and Zimbabwe, *shebeens* are most often located in black townships as an alternative to pubs and bars being reserved for white Africans during apartheid and the Rhodesian era. Originally, *shebeens* were operated illegally, selling home-brewed alcohol and providing patrons with a gathering place where they could meet and discuss political and social issues. Currently, *shebeens* are legal in South Africa and have become an integral part of its urban culture, serving commercial beers as well as *umqombothi*, a traditional African beer made from millet.

ROCKS. *Sphaphi* in the vernacular.

MOLOMO. The killer was getting braver—his previous victims had been shy and afraid of the night.

ROCKS. Quiet and almost innocent girls who were easy prey for him.

MOLOMO. A task team for the killings was formed and Rocks was assigned the lead detective.

ROCKS. The Behavioral Science Institute got involved and a psychologist drafted a profile of the killer.

MOLOMO. After studying the case material, she released the following profile . . .

A psychologist, Mantoa Nkhatho, comes through to recite the profile to the audience.

MISS NKHATHO. A young black male between the ages of 20 and 25. Of slender build. He most probably has a physical deformity or speech impediment . . . which is probably why he stalks his victims to this bushveld, instead of leading them here with his charisma . . . With other killers, like Moses Sithole, the victims actually trusted him . . . where—

ROCKS (*interrupts*). Moses Sithole promised them work, there was no business of "charisma" with him.

MISS NKHATHO. Whereas, with this one, I believe that . . . as a teenager, or in his pre-teens, he was probably teased or shunned by girls of his peer group. The killings are some sort of psychological revenge. And because of this, he probably didn't, and still doesn't, know how to speak to a girl.

ROCKS. Is it possible? I mean township boys think with their dicks. As far as I know, there's also—

MISS NKHATHO (*impatient*). Detective, can I please finish?

MOLOMO. Oh, come on, Rocks, let her finish. You'll give out your . . . your disagreements when she finishes.

ROCKS. Who's stopping her? (*To Miss Nkhatho*) Go on, go on. We have *real work* to do after you *theorize*.

MISS NKHATHO. It is my belief that he will never stop. He can't stop. He is starting to enjoy chasing after the girls. He gets some kind of a rush out of it . . . You must remember that . . . most serial killers were exposed to some sort of trauma in their formative years. Direct trauma, such as emotional, physical, and sexual abuse to the child. And, to escape the memories of their horror, they develop fantasies . . . violent fantasies, where they see themselves as aggressors instead of the victims they actually were. If a serial killer was severely beaten up by his parents as a child, he sometimes fantasizes about himself being the abuser. And when the fantasies reach a "boiling point," so to speak, a point where they cause unbearable inner stress, then the killer can be ready to act those fantasies out . . . In other words, he can be ready to kill. With this one, I think, by pure accident—I say "accident" because maybe he attacked the girl, his first attack probably, and because of inexperience on his part, the girl ran away . . . so he accidentally found pleasure or a thrill through chasing her . . . But the feeling of chasing someone around the bush like a lion chasing after its prey was so great that he has to re-live it every time he kills . . . he chases them around like wild game . . . to re-live and recreate the rush of the first chase . . . Therefore, it is my belief that the next killing will be in this very same location.

ROCKS. Night in, night out, we went on a useless stake-out . . . But the killer didn't strike.

MISS NKHATHO. He was on a cooling-off period. This is when a serial killer somehow manages to deal with his problems and doesn't see murder as his only solution. But it never lasts for long. Sooner or later, the urge to kill comes up again. Just as any alcoholic can never go for long without a drink, a serial killer never goes for long without killing.

MOLOMO. We turned the whole township upside down, interviewing everybody who fitted the suspect's description. But even with our 10-man task team, we were still too under-staffed to achieve a full and effective investigation.

ROCKS. But I remained forever optimistic that we would finally catch the bastard. These idiots cannot run forever. Sooner or later, they start making mistakes, careless mistakes . . . and I was confident that when this one made his inevitable mistake, we'd be right there to catch him.

MOLOMO. The first suspect we brought in for questioning was one Dario Sephai.

ROCKS. A first-class criminal . . . Well, not actually first-class in my eyes. He was one of those petty township criminals who get a hard-on out of terrorizing their communities. I dealt with many of his type every day. They have this boastful and brave exterior, trying to hide what cowards they actually are.

MOLOMO. Well, unlike my honorable partner here, I was actually not convinced that this Dario Sephai could be the serial killer.

ROCKS. I actually wanted a direct confession. Ever since I first started being a cop, I realized just how many people got away with murder, got away scot-free simply because the evidence wasn't enough . . . You see, what you have to understand about this country is how far behind we are, technologically speaking. We don't have all the hi-tech equipment and investigating devices that you find in movies or in the U.S. police services. Down here, if you don't get a confession, 90 percent of the time the suspect will walk.

Music . . . A handcuffed Dario (24 years) is hauled into the interrogation room by a uniformed cop, for the next beat.

Beat 2

The detectives approach him . . .

DARIO. I want my lawyer!

ROCKS. Lawyer *se gat!*[4] You think this is the movies?! Huh?! What do you know about lawyers?!

DARIO. I know I have my rights.

ROCKS. Not in here you don't! My job is to take all your rights away. You do the crime, you better be prepared to do the time.

DARIO. I didn't do anything!

ROCKS. You can't lie to me, boy! I have you already figured out. I'm more clever than you! I'm more clever than 20 of your brains put together. *Oska ntlela ka botsotsi ba twobob mo!*[5] Now listen here . . . I'm going to ask you certain questions . . . and I want nothing but the truth, otherwise you're going to find out why *ba mpitsa* Rocks![6]

DARIO. What questions?

ROCKS. Shut up! *Go botsa nna fela mo!*[7]

DARIO. *Jaanong ha go botsa wena fela,* Steve Urkell *ene o irang mo?*[8]

---

4 Arsehole.

5 Don't come with useless tricks to me!

6 . . . why I'm called Rocks!

7 I'm the only one that asks questions here!

8 Now if you're the only one that asks questions, what is Steve Urkell doing here?

MOLOMO. *Nna ke tla go fa mmago sani! Ke mang* Steve Urkell? *Hao na mokgwa he? Huh? Mmago ha go ruta maitseo?*[9] Huh?! (*Dario laughs at him*) *Oa tshega? Ke eng, o bona comediane mo?*[10] Huh?

DARIO. *Keng one o batla ke lle? Ha nka se lle grootman, wa nthuba!*[11]

MOLOMO. Rocks! *Ako o tswale seo se molomo se, ke tloga ke ntsha mabole yaanong nna! Kea mmona,*[12] he's looking for my "deadly uppercut!" . . .

Dario has the biggest laugh.

DARIO (*to Rocks*). Where do you get this joker? . . .

Rocks hits Dario.

ROCKS. I SAID, "I'M THE ONLY ONE THAT ASKS QUESTIONS HERE!"

MOLOMO. *Gata ntja*, Rocks! *Slaan hom!*[13]

DARIO. This is police brutality!

MOLOMO. *Mo gate*, Rocks![14] He can't even spell police brutality—even if you gave him a month to spell it!

ROCKS. Look at her. Are you looking?

DARIO. Yes.

ROCKS. Why did you kill her?

DARIO. *Ee, e, e, e* listen here, I don't know anything about her. I didn't kill her!

ROCKS. You're lying, *jou vuil pop*![15] You were seen beating her up in the street!

DARIO. What?!

ROCKS. Are you going to deny that?

MOLOMO. We have witnesses.

DARIO. But I didn't kill her.

---

9 I'll show you your mother, boy! Who's Steve Urkell? Don't you have any manners?

10 What you laughing at? What, you think I'm a comedian?

11 What, you want me to cry? I won't cry, old man, you're cracking me up!

12 Rocks! Please make him shut up, I'll start using my fists now! I can see, . . .

13 Hit the dog, Rocks! Beat him up!

14 Hit him, Rocks!

15 . . . you dirty bastard!

ROCKS. Now listen here . . . I've got three dead bodies, all strangled with a G-string . . . How many more are there?

DARIO. What?

ROCKS. How many more did you kill?!

DARIO. You think—*he banna*![16] You think I'm a serial killer? Three bodies? With a G-string? What are you saying? I'm not a serial killer, I haven't killed anybody.

MOLOMO. The night this girl died, she was with you.

DARIO. She wasn't with me.

MOLOMO. That's not what her friend says.

DARIO. I don't care what she says, she wasn't with me.

MOLOMO. *Fok jou!*[17] (*And then to Rocks . . .*) *Mo gate*, Rocks!

DARIO. No, wait . . . Okay . . . look . . . she came to my place, looking for me . . . I chased her away, I was with someone else. I was with my girlfriend, Matlakala. Why don't you ask her?

ROCKS. No, no, she won't work as your alibi. Obviously she's going to protect you. Think of a better lie.

MOLOMO. This girl, the dead girl . . . Sibongile Mabaso . . . you say you chased her away, what time was it?

DARIO. I don't know, it was late in the evening.

MOLOMO. And you chased her away, so that she can get killed?

ROCKS. Wait, wait, wait, Mouth . . . He didn't chase her away, she wasn't killed by anyone else . . . This arsehole *is* the killer . . . This is an open-and-shut case.

DARIO. I'm not a serial killer!

ROCKS. Listen here, I'm not going to play games with you. Just tell me why you killed her and the others.

DARIO. I didn't kill her! What's your problem? Didn't you hear me, I said—

Rocks hits him.

ROCKS. WHY DID YOU KILL HER?

---

16 —oh my God!

17 Fuck you!

DARIO. You can't beat me up like this, I have rights. I know the law. I can sue you for this!

ROCKS. The law doesn't apply on filth like you! Why did you kill her? (*Beat*) Are you going to answer me or do you first want me to light up your balls with a cigarette lighter? Mouth, give me a lighter—

MOLOMO. Don't call me Mouth!

ROCKS. Okay, Molomo . . . give me a cigarette lighter.

MOLOMO. *He banna! Laetara ya eng?*[18] You know I don't smoke.

ROCKS. Well, go out and get it for me.

MOLOMO. Me? Go out and get you a cigarette lighter?

ROCKS. That's what I said. This arsehole is going to confess if he doesn't want roasted balls.

MOLOMO. Wait a minute, Rocks . . . You don't outrank me. You can't send me like a *stuurboy*,[19] as if I'm your junior. I mean—

ROCKS. Fuck it, forget it, I'll get it myself.

Rocks goes out. Silence for a while. Molomo is looking at Dario.

DARIO. *Ee bona, hie—ka le chaela, sfebe sena ha sa bolaiwa ke nna.*[20] I didn't kill her! I mean—sure, I beat her up . . . yes, I admit that . . . *ek het haar vuil geskop, mara ha a bodiwa ke nna!*[21] And anyway, if I were to kill anyone I'd use a gun. I'm not a serial killer! I'm very normal, I'm not a mental case!

MOLOMO. It's not very normal to beat girls up!

DARIO. It's only this girl that I beat up. I found her fucking around behind my back! I mean, even yourself, what would you do?

MOLOMO. You have a history of abuse—you've been charged before for beating people up.

DARIO. Yes, well . . . uhm . . . I—listen . . . where I grew up . . . if you're not tough, if you don't hit first . . . people will play on your head. But I wouldn't kill anyone, most especially a girl . . .

---

18 Oh my God! Lighter? What for?

19 Errand boy.

20 Hey, look here . . . I'm telling you the truth, this bitch wasn't killed by me.

21 I kicked her to hell and back, but it wasn't me who killed her!

Beat. Molomo is pensive. Rocks comes back.

ROCKS. Take his pants off!

MOLOMO. What?

ROCKS. Take his pants off!

MOLOMO. Can we talk first?

ROCKS. Talk about what? Take his pants off, I got the matches—do your part!

MOLOMO. Can we talk in private first?

ROCKS. Talk about what?!

MOLOMO. Look, man, I don't think he did it.

ROCKS. We talked about this, let's not go back to that.

MOLOMO. But Rocks, we can't torture him. He didn't do it.

ROCKS. Whose side are you on? Were you there when this girl was killed?

MOLOMO. No, but—

ROCKS. Then don't say he didn't do it.

MOLOMO. But he doesn't fit the profile. He's not the serial-killer type!

ROCKS. Don't come and tell me about a profile, written by some woman who knows bugger-all about police work. I've been a cop for over 20 years! And anyway, if he didn't do it, we'll see after I burn his balls . . . This always works, he won't lie when his balls are being roasted like chicken, he'll tell the truth. Now come on, cuff him and let's take off his trousers.

Music. They manhandle him.

DARIO. Wait, wait, wait!

ROCKS. *Thula!*[22]

DARIO. I'm not a serial killer! I didn't do this!

ROCKS. *Mo tshware, mo tshware!*[23] Mouth!

They cuff him and take off his pants. They burn his balls. He screams and screams. After a while, the music pauses and Matlakala (16 or 17 years old) walks on to the stage. Matlakala is dressed in a school uniform and is holding a school bag—she is very, very drunk . . . She speaks directly to the audience.

---

22 Keep quiet!

23 Hold him, hold him!

MATLAKALA. Does anyone here know me? Is there anyone here who *thinks* he or she knows me? I'm not a philosopher or an analyst of life . . . I'm just a daughter of a bitch, just like any other son of a bitch inside this theater. I drink . . . I fuck . . . I lie . . . I eat . . . I smoke . . . I even go to church . . . sometimes. The only difference between me and you is that I can tell you my story. (*Beat*) And because it's *my* story . . . I can tell it whatever way I want . . . So . . . before we go on with the scene that follows this one . . . (*points behind her to the frozen Rocks and Dario and Molomo*), we're going to go back in time to several months earlier . . . Come to my house and hear all proper . . . hear angel trumpets and devil trombones . . . You are invited . . .

Music (the Beethoven used in Kubrick's A Clockwork Orange *during the high-speed sex scene). As the music comes up, the actors unfreeze and set up Beat Three, walking backwards very quickly.*

Beat 3

Several months earlier . . . At the Keagile house. Dan is in the kitchen. His wife, Dorah, comes through, following Matlakala. Matlakala comes on the stage with her luggage. Dorah is shouting at Matlakala.

DORAH. *He wena sekatana ke wena*,[24] where do you think you're going?!

MATLAKALA. Away! Away from you, away from your shouting, away from this house—

DORAH. And where do you think you're going to go?!

MATLAKALA. Don't worry yourself, *shem*.[25] Since when did you start caring?

DORAH (*grabs her angrily*). *O batla go reng*?! *Yeh*?! *O bua yang le nna*?![26]

MATLAKALA. *Ntlogele ke tsamaye tuu! Akere hao mpatle mo!*[27]

DORAH. Don't talk to me like *ke gamors fela, nna ke tlao klapa o nnyele* girl![28]

MATLAKALA (*ready to fight*). *O ka seke! Leka wena!*[29]

---

24 Hey, you tramp, . . .

25 Shame.

26 What?! Don't talk to me in that tone, girl!

27 Let me go, please! You don't want me in this house!

28 Don't talk to me like I'm rubbish, I'll hit you until you shit yourself . . . !

DORAH. *Heeee . . . Utlwang bathong*! Dan?! *Wa mo utlwa ngwana o wa gago?! O eme okare o sethotsela, o nchebile fela, hao nthuse!*[30]

DAN. My baby . . . why don't we sit down and talk about this?

MATLAKALA. There's nothing to talk about, Papa . . . *Ha a mpatle mo. Oa mo utlwa o mpitsa sekatana.*[31]

DORAH. *O eng wena?! Hao bone gore o sone. Hao bone gore o iphetotse stratmeit! Ore keng, o nagana gore o mosadi?! Ha se gore hao kreya di-phiriote o mosadi.*[32]

MATLAKALA. *Oa mo utlwa,*[33] Papa.

DAN. *Dorah, lwena ako o eme pele*[34] man!

DORAH. *He-e Dan*! Don't you dare! Don't you dare take her side! *Ke wena o mo senyang ngwana o! Nna ha ke batle ngwana o tlong tlelang ka bofebe ba ko straateng!*[35]

MATLAKALA. *Ha ke sfebe!*[36]

DORAH. *O setse o itse polo yanong, ebile e go ruta le gore o inkarabisetse!*[37] And I'm telling you, my girl, you'll never amount to anything in life! You'll end up exactly like this . . . what you are . . . *kuku e e dulang e emetse go jewa!*[38]

MATLAKALA (*tearfully*). It's okay, it's okay . . .

DAN. *Ngwanaka,*[39] running away won't solve anything. I mean, where will you go? *Kaosane re tla be re utlwa gotwe o* prostitute *yanong*[40] . . . Please stay, my baby . . . we can overcome this, you'll get over this . . . Let's sort out our

---

29 Never! Just try!

30 Heeee . . . Just listen to that! Dan?! Do you hear this child of yours?! You're just standing there like a zombie without helping me!

31 She doesn't want me here. You heard her, she's calling me a tramp.

32 What're you?! Don't you see you are a tramp! You've turned yourself into a streetmate! Or what, you think you're a woman now?! If you get periods, it doesn't mean you're a woman.

33 You hear that, . . .

34 Dorah, wait a minute . . .

35 No, Dan! . . . You're spoiling this child! I don't want a child to come to me with her street-whoring!

36 I'm not a whore!

37 You already know a dick now, it's even teaching you to answer back to me!

38 . . . a vagina that's always waiting to be fucked!

39 My child . . .

problems like civilized human beings without screaming about like . . . like we're coloreds *ba ko*[41] Eldorado Park . . .

DORAH. Dan, *nna o satlo mpitsa le-khalati!*[42] . . . I'm not a colored *nna!*[43] Put some sense into this daughter of yours. *Kgante wena,*[44] what kind of a man are you?

DAN. Now you're getting out of line, Dorah . . . You can't talk to me like that in front of the child.

DORAH. *Ke reng nna?*[45] It's your daughter you should be talking to, not me. You're behaving like you're a man only by what hangs between your legs!

DAN. Don't push me, Dorah, don't push me to do something I'll regret!

DORAH. What are you talking about? Your whole life is full of regrets! What, am I too wrong to speak my mind?! You only become a man when you go to the toilet and masturbate.

DAN. Dorah, *o tla tloga o ntena, ke tla tloga ke go khenekha yanong,*[46] strue's God!

DORAH (*laughing sarcastically*). Heeee! He-he-he! You?! Hit me?! With what?! You can't afford it, man. You're unemployed! You can't afford the medical bills or your bail for that matter! You're useless, Dan—you're just like this rubbish daughter of yours.

MATLAKALA. *Nna ha ke* rubbish *nna!* You're a very bad woman, *ebile ha ke itse go tlile yang gore* Papa *ago nyale!*[47]

DORAH (*slaps her*). Hei, *voetsek! O mpotsa masepa, jou fokon* bitch! *Tswa, tswa!*[48] Get out of my bloody house!

MATLAKALA. I was going anyway! (*Leaves, with her bags.*)

---

40 Tomorrow we'll start hearing that you're a prostitute . . .

41 . . . from . . .

42 Dan, don't come and call me a colored!

43 Me/myself.

44 What about you, . . .

45 What should I say?

46 Dorah, you're starting to piss me off, and I'll beat you up, . . .

47 I'm not a rubbish! You're a very bad woman, I don't even know how it came about that Papa married you!

48 Fuck off! You're telling me shit, you fucking bitch! Get out, get out!

DORAH. Go, go! *Re tla bona gore o tla fella kae*! And don't ever come here! *Le ka tsatsi la motlholo*! *Jou fokon* bitch![49]

Matlakala runs off. Dario's shack is set up . . .

Beat 4

Dario is with his two friends—Pelo (20 years) and Mavarara (22 years). They are sitting in a street corner, smoking weed and talking.

DARIO. *Ek het daai* bitch *vuil geskop! Vuil, vuil, vuil! Go tswa daar ko Mamiki's ne ke mo mathisa mo strateng moen my parabellum tot-tot gore le kuku ya gage ya* "one for all" *ebe e fufule*.[50]

PELO. *Hae, o masepa ntanga . . .* Dario *kai* one, *kai* two *ke mo fothong*! I heard that story, *bla yaka*![51]

MAVARARA. *Watte cherrie is daai?*[52]

DARIO. That bitch called Sibongile.

MAVARARA. Oooh, that one who didn't want you to fuck her the other day?

DARIO. *Ja, die selde snaai. Le daai tyd a neng a ntshokodisa ke sele ka mo chuma met 'n warm klap ebe ke mo isa gae. Ha ke tlo ncenga nnyo nna!*[53] . . .

PELO. *Ha mare, jy't haar vuil ge-skop Ntanga*! I saw her yesterday *ka daar ka ko strateng sa bone*[54] . . . I didn't even recognize her—if it wasn't for that *unique* arse of hers, I wouldn't have known her. You've really reorganized her face, even those sunglasses she had on couldn't hide her ugliness—*omo kobofaditse ntanga*![55]

---

49 Go, go! And don't ever come here! Even if hell freezes over! You fucking bitch!

50 I gave that bitch a thorough beating! I gave her a chase with my parabellum from Mamiki's until that "one for all" pussy of her got all sweaty.

51 You're a bad arse, my friend . . . Dario only once, for the second time it's only on a photo! I heard that story my friend . . .

52 Which "chick" is that?

53 Yes, the very whore. Even that time when she didn't want to give out, I hit her with a hot slap and then took her home. I won't beg for pussy!

54 You gave her a filthy beating, my friend! I saw her yesterday at the street where she lives . . .

55 —you've really made her ugly, my friend!

DARIO. *Wa nkitse, wa nkitse!*[56]

MAVARARA. *Ele gore* why *omo murile?*[57] What did she do to you?

DARIO. *Ne, o ntlwaela masepa daai hoermeit!*[58] I go there *ko* Mamiki's[59] and I find her hanging out with some arsehole—'n charma-boy wannabe . . . They were hugging and laughing as if they're in "The Bold and The Beautiful."

MAVARARA. *Kak! Kak!* The Bold *se gat! Ke kasi hieso!*[60]

DARIO. When I went over there, where they were sitting, and I told that bitch we must go, she answered me like shit, *a ntlolela okare*[61] popcorn. And *daai moegoe*[62] says to me, "You heard the lady, she doesn't want to go" . . . *ka sekgowanyana sa matsatsantsa!*[63] I hit him with a flying kick before he could even stand up!

Pelo laughs excitedly.

PELO. I know you *ntanga.*[64] *Jean Clodi Van Deim!*[65]

DARIO. When he was still trying to recover from my kick, I stepped on his chest, with my nine mm already out!

PELO. *E, e, e . . . o mmontshitse* movie *wena mos?*[66]

DARIO. Now, as I was turning to deal with the bitch, I find out she's gone! I went after her! When I caught her, *ek het hom haar ma ge chee. Hierso, bo di hand. Ha kao chaela, ke mo trapile dik, ka mo tlisa hie, ka mo nyoba dik!*[67]

Mavarara laughs at that.

---

56 You know me, you know me!

57 Why did you beat her up?

58 She takes me for shit, that whore!

59 . . . from Mamiki's . . .

60 Crap! Crap! Fuck "the Bold"! We're in the township here!

61 . . . jumping about like . . .

62 . . . that idiot . . .

63 . . . with a coconut English!

64 . . . my friend.

65 You're Jean Claude Van Damme!

66 You showed him a movie?

67 . . . I beat her up. I'm telling you, I beat her up like crazy, and then I brought her here, and I fucked her like crazy!

PELO. *Ha mare, Ma-D, nke sele wa mo gana*! Bullet-out, *binne bo daai koek*![68]

DARIO. *Hae, nnyo hae ganiwe, bafo, ya jewa*! *Ya jewa daai ding*! *Ee,* die man! That's why *o bolaiwa ke go iskomora so*![69] (*Matlakala comes through from the opposite side of the street, carrying her bags. Mavarara is the first to see her and he pokes Dario to look. Dario is surprised to see her. He rises and slowly approaches her as she approaches him . . .*) And then? *Wat gat aan ka di beke*?[70] (*She is crying. She drops her bags, looking for pity . . .*) *Wat nou*? What *jive*?[71]

MATLAKALA. *Ba nkobile ko gae*.[72]

DARIO. *Ba go kobile*?[73] (*He is surprised and doesn't know what to say.*)

Matlakala turns to face the audience . . .

MATLAKALA (*to the audience*). What we do in the name of love . . . I was 15 when I first met Dario. He told me that he loved me, and . . . that I meant the whole world to him. He called me his bitch, *sfebe sa gage*[74] . . . He was my love, my one and only . . . I gave up my family in the name of love. I gave up my friends, my future, my everything . . . all in the name of love. (*She and Dario kiss as the setting is changed to Dario's bedroom. They get on the bed as they begin foreplay. But before it gets far, Matlakala stops him . . .*) Dario?

DARIO. Huh?

MATLAKALA. Wait a minute . . .

DARIO. Huh?

MATLAKALA. Wait a minute . . . We can't do this without a condom.

DARIO. What do you mean? *O batlo o reng eintlek*?[75]

MATLAKALA. Do you have condoms?

DARIO. *Ei, ne dile teng daai goetes dibodile*.[76]

---

68 But Dario, you should've shot her! Bullet-out, right inside her cunt!

69 You don't shoot a pussy, man, you fuck it! This guy . . . that's why you wank all the time!

70 What's going on with the bags?

71 What now? What's the problem?

72 They chased me away from home.

73 They chased you away?

74 . . . his bitch . . .

75 What are you trying to say?

MATLAKALA. What?

DARIO. *Di fedile.*[77]

MATLAKALA. What do you mean? It means you sleep with other people.

DARIO. There's no one else, it's only you. I gave Mavarara my last pack of condoms. Now come on, don't spoil the mood, let's do this . . .

MATLAKALA. No, Dario. It's not safe, you sleep with too many girls. If I sleep with you without a condom, I'll be sleeping with all those other girls.

DARIO. What other girls? *O batlo reng mara ye?*[78] There's no other girls! Look, I don't know where you get these crazy ideas but . . . to tell you the truth, I'm getting fed up—*o tlo nkhenya go sa le* early.[79] You're the only one I sleep with.

MATLAKALA. I'm not stupid, Dario. *Kea itse ka* Itebeng[80] . . . She told me about you . . . I also know that you fuck Pulane, so please don't lie.

DARIO. Okay, okay, I admit, I did fuck Itebeng, but I was drunk . . . she's the one who seduced me . . . and anyway, we were not that serious by then, me and you . . . But Pulane *ene, o bua mmage*[81] if she says I fucked her!

MATLAKALA. Yes, but I can't afford to be pregnant, Dario. I have to go to school.

DARIO. You won't be pregnant, baby, *otla spanisa di*-morning-after.[82] And please don't tell me about school, coz it's two months since you've gone to school . . . and you know you don't like it.

MATLAKALA. There's this girl at school, she's pregnant now . . . she used *di*-morning-after and she's pregnant now.

DARIO. She didn't use them correctly. *Sy's dom! Ke sho ene o di spanisitse leite, ka bo ma* afternoon *ore* after two days, *ore bosigo bo bo latelang—ene daai ding tsele di bitswa di* "morning-after," *eseng di* "afternoon-after" *ore di* "night-after" *ore di* "two-days after"[83] . . . (*Matlakala has a laugh, despite herself.*) Now come on, we'll argue about this later.

---

76 They were here, those things, but I'm out now.

77 They're finished.

78 What are you trying to say?

79 —you are going to piss me off very quickly.

80 I know about Itebeng . . .

81 But Pulane, she's fucking lying . . .

82 . . . you'll use morning-after pills.

Music . . . Dario kisses her passionately. They continue making love. This is repre-
sented in a non-naturalistic way—as a kind of dance during the scene change.

Dario gets an artificial tummy and puts it—as part of the "dance"—under Mat-
lakala's dress. After this, she walks to the center of the stage, a pregnant woman hold-
ing her tummy thoughtfully. The lights dim, leaving a spot on her.

MATLAKALA (*to the audience*). I lived together with Dario *mo mpantjeng wa gage.*[84]
A matchbox shack full of stolen goods. I had everything a girl could want.
If I needed anything, Dario would simply steal it for me. Nothing was im-
possible for him. (*Beat*) It was at this point in my story that Dario got
arrested . . . He was accused of being a serial killer and his balls were burnt
. . . Lucky for him, he had already got me pregnant.

Rocks and Molomo come through and call out Dario's name.

ROCKS. Dario Sephai?

DARIO. Yes?

ROCKS. Detective Motshegare.

MOLOMO. Detective Molomo.

Dario instantly runs, thinking that they want him in connection with one of his many
robberies . . . They chase him, off the stage . . . A pregnant Matlakala runs after them,
shouting out to Dario.

Beat 5

After the song fades, we find Dan sitting with Lungi. Mamiki, the shebeen owner, is
arguing with Dan about how Dan still owes her . . . After a while, Mamiki goes away.
Lungi is reading a newspaper. There is a girl called Pulane seated with another girl at
a different table. At yet another table is a young man (Thabo) reading a book and drink-
ing coffee.

LUNGI. Hei, look here my friend . . . They say the G-string Strangler has
claimed Victim Number Four . . .

DAN. Number Four? He's getting busy . . .

---

83 She's stupid! I'm sure she used them late in the afternoon or after two days, or the following evening—and those things are called "morning-after" pills, not "afternoon-after"
or "night-after" or "two-days-after" . . .

84 . . . in his shack.

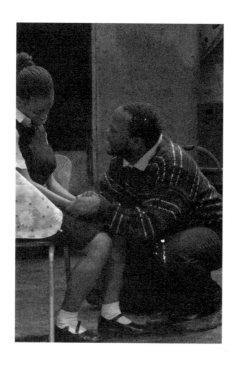

ABOVE: *Refilwe Mokgotlhoa (Matlakala)*
and Mahlubi Kraai (Dan).
BELOW: *Karabo Kgokong (Dario) and*
Refilwe Mokgotlhoa (Matlakala).
Photograph by Mpumelelo Paul Grootboom.

ABOVE: *Refilwe Mokgotlhoa (Matlakala)*.
BELOW: *Zenzo Nqobe (Thabo)*.
Photograph by Mpumelelo Paul Grootboom.

FROM LEFT TO RIGHT: *Fumani Shilubana* (*Extra*) *and Presley Chweneyagae* (*Extra*).

LUNGI. Why do you think this happens? . . . I mean, someone going around killing people like this?

DAN. I don't know, *bot*,[85] that question should be directed to God, not me. All I know is, I hope they catch him . . . coz my daughter is out there where I don't know . . .

A song comes up softly: Satchmo's "Cheek to Cheek."

LUNGI. *Ag*,[86] don't worry, they always catch them in the end. *Mina*,[87] I don't know why—

DAN (*interrupting*). Listen . . . listen, my friend . . .

LUNGI. What?

DAN. The song, the song . . . You know, this song . . . this song *e nkgopotsa* the first time *ke kopana le* Dorah . . . We were very young then . . . She was very beautiful, she still is . . . But that time, *eish*,[88] *bot* . . . *kaochaela* man . . . that woman was a marvel! *Lerago lele, bot, dirope tsele, bot, matswele ale, bot . . . ijooo, hao itse niks wena! Marcia Turner bot!*[89] (*He shouts out to the back*) Hei Mamiki, Mamiki?! Volume, give me some volume, doll!

The volume goes up and Dan begins dancing. He goes into a flashback-like sequence, where we see him dancing with Dorah like an ace. At a certain point, Dorah moves off and Dan is left standing there like a zombie, as if telling us that that time is now over.

LUNGI (*crossing to him*). Dan?! Danille? Dan?!

Dan snaps out of his trance-like state when Lungi shakes him.

DAN. It's all gone now . . . It's gone . . . The music is over . . .

LUNGI. Cheer up, man, things will come right.

DAN. Come right *kae, bot*? . . . I've gone through six months without getting any. *Okare ke mo traeleng ko* New Lock.[90] I last ejaculated when I lost my job.

---

85 . . . brother, . . .

86 Oh, . . .

87 Me, . . .

88 Used in South African English and Afrikaans to express exasperation or dibelief.

89 . . . this song reminds me of the first time I met up with Dorah . . . But that time . . . *eish*, brother, I'm telling you, man . . . that woman was a marvel! That arse . . . those thighs . . . those breasts. You know nothing, you. Marcia Turner, brother!

LUNGI. *Shapa ma*-dice, my friend. *Shaya ma*-dice. *Mina*, that's what I do.[91]

DAN. I'm tired of masturbating, *bot*! Plus they say it makes you blind.

LUNGI. *Eee?* Is that true? I've been feeling my eyes going bad . . .

DAN. I don't know what happened, *bot* . . . (*He starts to cry*) What happened to this woman? What happened to her motherly love . . . huh? Her compassion, her . . . her . . . *eish*, *bot*! . . . It's all so . . . so complicated. (*He cries and cries.*)

LUNGI. Take it easy, man . . . It's not the end of the world. Things will come right . . . Come on, my friend, don't cry . . . don't cry . . . (*He tries to speak Tswana; he has a heavy Zulu accent*) *Mutlugele, mudimu utla mmona*[92] . . .

They move off and go home. Dan takes the beer bottle from Lungi as they start out . . . Just then, Mamiki appears.

MAMIKI. Heey, Dan! That's my empty!

DAN. It's still full, my doll . . . I'll bring it tomorrow.

MAMIKI. And if you don't come with my money tomorrow, don't bother to come at all!

DAN. *Tlogela bo-snakse*, man![93]

MAMIKI. *Hai tsamaya!*[94]

DAN (*as he exits*). *O snakse* man! *O snaks! O snaks!*[95]

After Dorah, Lungi, and Dan exit, Mamiki is left alone with one patron (Thabo, 19 years). She approaches him; he has been immersed in his reading . . .

MAMIKI. And then, *wena?*[96]

THABO (*raising his head*). Huh?

MAMIKI. Why are you still here? I'm closing up.

---

90 What do you mean "come right?" I've gone through six months without getting any. It's as if I'm on a trial in New Lock Prison.

91 Play the dice, my friend. Play the dice. Me, that's what I do.

92 Leave her be, God will deal with her . . .

93 Stop being funny, man!

94 Go away!

95 You are funny, funny, funny!

96 . . . you.

THABO. I'm still finishing my coffee.

MAMIKI. Your coffee? This is a tavern, you know. Why do you want to drink coffee in a tavern?

THABO. I like being around people.

MAMIKI. Well, people are gone. You can go too.

THABO. As soon as I finish my coffee. I paid for it.

Mamiki surveys him in silence for a while.

MAMIKI. You know, I've seen you around here . . . You say you like people, but I've never seen you talking to anyone.

THABO. I said, "I like *being around* people." I never said, "I like people."

Beat.

MAMIKI. You sound intelligent. What are you reading?

THABO. *Jack and the Beanstalk.*

MAMIKI. Ooh, I see . . . we have Bill Cosby here.

THABO. I'm not joking, it's the truth.

MAMIKI. Let me see.

THABO. No, you won't like it . . . It's a pornographic novel, not the common fairy tale . . . The beanstalk is Jack's phallic instrument, you know, ehm—

MAMIKI. Spare me the details. (*Sits down and lights a cigarette*) What's your name?

THABO. Thabo.

MAMIKI. You sound like someone very intelligent. Are you a university scholar or anything like that?

THABO. Anything like that.

MAMIKI. I was a scholar myself . . . Didn't finish though . . . And now, look at what I am . . . A doctor of the liquor business. (*Beat*) Why do you read pornography? Do you have a girlfriend? (*He hands her the book*) It's not pornography at all . . . *Catcher in the Rye* . . . J. D. Salinger . . . I've never seen this one before.

THABO. Famous book.

MAMIKI. So . . . do you or don't you?

THABO. Don't what?

MAMIKI. Have a girl.

THABO. No, I've never met anyone good for me . . . (*Thuli walks in . . . Aside*) Until now.

THULI. Mama, *ke ilo robala*.[97]

MAMIKI. Sharp, my baby. Goodnight. Come on, give me a hug . . .

As she stands to hug Thuli, everybody except Thabo freezes.

THABO. There was nothing really special about her . . . But, from that moment, I could write 10 to 40 poems about this girl . . . She was oozing with purity, cleanliness, something you just want to lock away in Consol glass and observe and scrutinize for eternity . . . My Eve minus the Forbidden Fruit . . .

They unfreeze and hug.

MAMIKI. Night.

THULI. Night, Ma. (*Thuli moves off.*)

MAMIKI. That's my daughter, you know.

THABO. What?

MAMIKI. I saw you. That look . . . I don't like it.

THABO. If you don't want us to look at her, you should stop her from working in such a place.

MAMIKI. She's everything to me. I want her to be the best of what I could never be.

THABO. You must really love her.

MAMIKI. Yes, that I do. She's a gem. So stay away from her. (*Beat*) How old are you?

THABO. Nineteen.

MAMIKI. You're younger than I thought.

THABO. How old are you?

MAMIKI. Don't you know you're not supposed to ask a lady such a question?

THABO. You must be 50 then.

MAMIKI. Oh no—50? How cruel. How can you choose such an age for me?

---

97 Mama, I'm going to sleep.

THABO. How old then?

MAMIKI. Let's just say I'm way younger than 50 . . . and way older than my daughter. (*Beat*) What about some music, Mr. Academic?

THABO. Music?

MAMIKI. Yes . . .

THABO. Sure.

Music comes up. Marvin Gaye's "Sexual Healing." Mamiki dances seductively.

MAMIKI. You know, when this song plays . . . it takes me far, far away, to special places . . . When it plays, I just feel . . . this feeling . . .

THABO. What feeling?

MAMIKI. Of dancing with the right man. Come on, come on, let's dance.

THABO. No . . .

MAMIKI. Come on . . . Don't be shy. I'll lead you. Come on, humor me . . . (*She manages to get him dancing. They dance and then she kisses him. He is highly surprised. She is panting, though. She kisses him passionately. He decides to fall into it. She throws him on the chair and tears her blouse open.*)

THABO. Wait a minute.

MAMIKI. Shhhhhh . . . don't speak! (*She climbs on top of him and kisses him again. She stands up after a while and begins undressing him until he is in only his shorts and vest.*)

The bed is moved to a more central position and Mamiki's bedroom is set up. We now have both the shebeen *area and the bedroom on stage. Mamiki and Thabo go into the bedroom and they fuck under the sheets.*

After the fucking, Mamiki gets out of bed and puts on her morning gown.

MAMIKI. *Shuu* . . . That was . . . that was something else . . . I think I need a cigarette. (*She has a smoke. She looks at him for a while*) *Mara wa itse gore o monate byang?*[98] (*He says nothing*) But don't let that go to your head. It's nothing you did. It's just . . . actually, I don't know what it is . . . Maybe your thing, it's not big that it can hurt, and yet . . . it's not small that it can tickle . . . It's just . . . "perfect." A perfect fit. Or maybe it's not your thing . . . It's you . . . Maybe you're just perfect . . . A perfect . . . fit. Huh? I was married, you

---

98 Do you know how delicious you are?

know. Divorced now. There was just something in that marriage that nearly made me hate sex. But now . . . I remember why it's such a—

Thuli's voice comes from offstage.

THULI. Mama? (*She throws Thabo off the bed, to the side where he won't be seen. Thuli walks in*) Mama?

MAMIKI. I told you to knock before you come in here!

THULI. There's someone at the door. It's the police. They want to speak to you.

MAMIKI. What do they want?

THULI. I don't know.

MAMIKI. *Ag*, they must catch this killer and stop bothering me!

THULI. What must I tell them, then?

MAMIKI. Okay, okay, let's go, let's go.(*She walks off with Thuli.*)

Music.

THABO. What a talker . . . I knew it right away: she was in love with me, and here I was, in love with her daughter . . . There's a psychological term for people who sleep with someone just because they want to get closer to someone else who happens to be closest to that someone . . . Maybe that's what was happening to me, I thought at that moment . . . I had slept with the mother just to get closer to her daughter . . . I don't know what the term for that is, but I'll call that "alternative affection" . . . That's what my father suffered from . . .

The lights dim in Mamiki's bedroom and come up in the shebeen *area. Mamiki is talking to the detectives.*

MAMIKI. This is a classy place, Detective . . . I serve only the best-mannered people.

ROCKS. Manners and alcohol don't go together.

MISS NKHATHO. We believe the killer may be one of your clients, and we're here to see if—

MAMIKI (*interrupting*). My clients? I serve only the best. This is a classy place.

MISS NKHATHO. Why, do you know *all* your clients?

MAMIKI. Not all, but I know most of them.

MISS NKHATHO. There you go . . . You see, you can't control whoever comes in here. A killer could come in here unseen.

ROCKS (*impatient, upstaging Miss Nkhatho*). Look, lady, just supply us with the names and addresses of all your clients so that we can talk to them!

MAMIKI. Do you have a warrant?

ROCKS. A warrant? For what? Listen here, woman, we don't need a warrant to get names from you . . . Either you give us the names or we detain you for a while until you give them up.

MAMIKI. That would be police harassment. I'm well-versed with the law.

ROCKS. Look here, you don't want to be telling us about warrants . . . If I have to come with a warrant, I'll come with a lot more warrants for many other criminal activities that go on in your place . . .

MAMIKI. I have nothing to hide. And I'm not scared of the police . . . My ex-husband used to be one. If you don't have a warrant, then get the hell out of my place before I sue you for trespassing and police harassment.

MOLOMO (*trying to intervene*). No, no, listen—

ROCKS (*to Mamiki*). Are you threatening me?! Coz if you are, I'll arrest you, right now, on the spot!

MAMIKI. I'm not scared of you, Detective!

MOLOMO. Rocks, wait!

ROCKS (*threatening, overlapping Molomo*). You're not scared of me?

MOLOMO. Rocks, please, let me handle this.

ROCKS. There's nothing to handle, Mouth. This woman thinks—

MOLOMO. Wait, wait! Rocks, you're not making things easy for us. Please, stay back . . . I'll handle this.

MAMIKI. Look, I'm not giving you any names. Come with a warrant before you talk to me. This a classy place, I don't serve killers here!

MOLOMO. I know, I know, but—

ROCKS. Let's just arrest this slut and get the names from—

MAMIKI. Hey, hey, I'm not a slut! Who are you calling a slut?! Go and call your whoring wife a slut!

ROCKS (*charging her, offended*). What?!

MOLOMO (*blocking him off*). No, no, Rocks, wait!

MISS NKHATHO (*overlapping with Rocks*). What is this now?

ROCKS (*overlapping with Miss Nkhatho*). Did you just call my wife a slut? (*To Molomo*) Let me go, Mouth!

MOLOMO. No, no, but wait, Rocks . . . You called her a slut first.

ROCKS. She *is* a slut. She's a bitch. What's wrong with calling her what she is?

MAMIKI. Hey, *mina* I'm not a bitch! It's your wife you're talking about! Your wife, your mother, your grandmother all combined together! Go call them bitches before—

Rocks lunges at her before she can continue and grabs her by the throat . . . He has already drawn his gun and has put it to her head.

ROCKS. Do you know my wife?! Do you know my wife?!

MOLOMO (*trying to pull Rocks back*). No, Rocks, no . . . Put the gun down.

MISS NKHATHO (*also trying to help*). Detective, let her go!

MOLOMO. Back off, Rocks!

ROCKS. Do you know who my wife is, you fucking bitch?! Huh?! Do you know her?!

MOLOMO. Let her go, Rocks . . . Please!

Just then, Thabo walks in. Rocks is shocked to see him.

ROCKS. Thabo? (*He lets go of Mamiki. Thabo passes them, picking up his steps as he goes . . .*) Thabo?!

As Thabo runs off, Rocks runs after him . . . It is as though Rocks has seen a ghost.

MISS NKHATHO. Who's that?

MOLOMO. I think . . . I think it's his son.

MAMIKI (*surprised*). His son?

MISS NKHATHO (*to Mamiki*). Are you okay?

MAMIKI (*pushing her off in anger*). I'm fine, I'm fine!

MISS NKHATHO (*to Molomo*). Jesus! What's his problem? (*Molomo starts out . . . Miss Nkhatho follows him*) He's a mental case—he shouldn't be in charge of such an investigation . . .

Music for scene change.

Beat 6

Flashback . . .

A montage of shots relating Thabo's story from birth to when he's around 13 years old:

1. We see Rocks and his pregnant wife, Mihloti, in their loving (flowery) moments. Mihloti suddenly goes into labor and Rocks takes her to the bed to deliver the baby.

2. The doctors come through after Rocks puts Mihloti on the bed. Mihloti is screaming as the two doctors help her deliver. They shout and shout "push–push." After they remove the artificial belly, a smiling Rocks emerges from behind the bed with his infant son, Thabo . . . The artificial belly has been switched for the actor playing Thabo.

3. Rocks and Mihloti move forward to center stage, as they play with the infant son in Rocks's hands. Rocks puts the boy down and the boy starts to crawl away, like a one-year-old baby.

4. When the boy comes back to Rocks and Mihloti, he is now starting to walk. Rocks catches the boy before he falls. Mihloti moves away to get a tricycle for the child (who is now around three or four). She gives the tricycle to the boy and the boy moves off to play with friends. Thabo's friends are playing cars with beer crates around the stage.

5. When Thabo comes back, his family moves to center spot and they begin miming a ride in a car. Thabo's childhood friends play around with the crates, and when, they crash the crates together, Thabo's family falls over—as if in a car crash.

6. Rocks rises from the wreckage and picks up his wife (the only one seriously wounded) and takes her to the bed, where doctors attend to her. They cover her with a white cloth and put her on a stretcher. As they move offstage with her, Rocks and Thabo are crying for her.

The scene is then transformed for the following beat. It is important to note that all actors in the cast are involved in this scene change. They remove tables as if they are children playing with car wheels, etc.

Thirteen-year-old Thabo is being interrogated by his father, Rocks, in their house.

ROCKS. Thabo?

THABO (*scared*). Papa?

ROCKS. What's going on?

THABO. Papa?

ROCKS. *Ke go botsa potso* man! *Keng, hao nkutlwe?*[99]

THABO. *Kea go utlwa,*[100] Papa.

ROCKS. Then answer me . . . What's going on with you?

THABO. What's going with what, Papa?

ROCKS. I was with your teacher today––MaKutu. She was complaining about you. She says you show no attention at all in your schoolwork. She says you sometimes sleep in class, and that you're always absent-minded, and that you're failing your tests. She also says you're the brightest kid in the school and if this goes on, you're soon going to be the dullest . . . a dunderhead . . . 'n domkop . . . And *ha kena ngwana wa domkop nna . . . Keng*?! *Hao batle skolo*?![101]

THABO. *He-e*[102] Papa.

ROCKS (*fiercely*). *Yeh, ore he-e*?![103]

THABO (*sobbing*). *He-e* Papa, *ha kere he-e, ka se batla*, Papa.[104]

ROCKS. *Yanong keng*? What the hell is going on?! *Keng okare otla iphetola setlhoko tsebe yana? Heh*?![105] (*Thabo is crying*) Stop it! Stop it, *o llelang*?! Huh?! Are you a girl?! *O shapilwe ke mang*?! *Ore o batla ke go shape gore o lle sentle*?![106]

THABO. *He-e*.

ROCKS. *Yanong keng*?![107] Why are you crying?! Huh?! Thabo?!

THABO. Papa?

ROCKS. I'm talking to you!

THABO. Papa?

ROCKS. Why are you crying?!

THABO. Papa *akere wena ha ke bala o tla mo gonna,*[108] . . . and . . . and . . . you hurt me . . . *o nkutlwisa botlhoko kana she*[109] . . . Sometimes, sometimes when I

---

99 I'm asking you a question, man! What, don't you hear me?!

100 I hear you, . . .

101 And I don't have a dunderhead for a child. What, don't you want to go to school any more?!

102 No . . .

103 What, did you just say—no?!

104 No Papa, I didn't say no. I want it, Papa.

105 Now what? What the hell is going on? Why are you turning yourself into a problem child?!

106 Stop it! Stop it, what are you crying for?! Are you girl? Who hit you?! Or do you want me to hit you so that you can cry for the right thing?

107 Now what?!

think of coming home, I get . . . I get this feeling . . . this feeling of not coming home . . . MaKutu always asks me what's wrong and . . . and I feel like telling her . . . I feel like telling her the truth . . . *gore wena o nkutlwisa botlhoko ha ke robetse . . . gore wa ntshwara*[110] . . . and I don't like how you touch me . . . and . . . that you don't . . . you don't love me . . .

ROCKS. Okay, okay, Big Boy . . .

THABO. *Hao nrate,*[111] Papa—

ROCKS. *Ha se jalo*[112] "the Great" . . . Please *chana*[113] man . . . Don't go telling people that I don't love you . . . telling them about these things . . . you haven't told her anything, have you?

THABO. *Mh-hm* Papa. *Ha ka molella, mara . . . mara . . .*[114]

ROCKS. Easy *chana* . . . it's not that I don't love you, my boy . . . it's just that Papa *o misa*[115] Mama . . . Do you understand? . . . Huh? . . . You know I wouldn't hurt you . . . I just forget myself . . . I miss your mother too much . . . I can't bear the thought that I'll never see her again . . . I'm always waiting for her but she never comes . . .

THABO. *He-e* Papa, please don't touch me . . .

Music. The apparition of Mihloti walks in.

ROCKS. Easy, Big Boy . . . You know I love you. It's just that I miss your mother. I miss everything about her. I miss her cooking, her smile, her eyes . . . her voice. (*To Mihloti*) Howzit baby?

MIHLOTI. Hallo, my love?

ROCKS. Oooh, it's so good to see you again.

MIHLOTI. Yes, yes, same here, my pumpkin . . .

---

108 Papa, when I sleep you come to me and again you hit me, . . .

109 . . . oh, you are hurting me . . .

110 . . . that you hurt me when I'm sleeping . . . that you touch me . . .

111 You don't love me, . . .

112 It's not like that . . .

113 Also, China. Slang term of endearment as in "my friend."

114 No Papa. I didn't tell her, but . . . but . . .

115 Misses—here slang term for "woman."

ROCKS. And your voice, too . . . Oh, it's wonderful to hear it . . . Why did you have to go, baby? Why?

MIHLOTI. I'm not gone . . . I'm with you. I'll always be with you. (*She starts to move back, starting out of the stage.*)

ROCKS. Mihloti? Don't go!

MIHLOTI. I love you.

ROCKS. Don't go . . . Mihloti! (*By this time he is fondling Thabo.*)

THABO. Papa? Papa? Please don't touch me like this . . .

ROCKS (*simultaneously*). Mihloti? Mihloti? Mihloti, please don't go like this . . . (*But Mihloti is gone . . . Thabo snaps his father out of this trance. Music ends abruptly. Thabo has stood up from the chair and is now standing away from his father.*) Sorry, sorry, Big Boy. I didn't mean it . . . I'm so sorry . . . I'll never do it again . . . You don't need to tell anyone about this. Not even your teacher, MaKutu. She doesn't need to know coz Papa is going to search for help. I'll never do this to you again. Now come, go to sleep, there's school tomorrow . . . *Ala o robale.*[116]

Music . . . Thabo prepares his blankets. He undresses until he is in his jockeys and gets under the blankets to sleep. A tormented Rocks is in the background, looking worriedly at a distance. When the boy is snoring, Rocks approaches him. When he's standing over the boy, a tear drops down his cheek. He begins to undress himself until he is in his BVDs. He slowly gets under the blankets with Thabo, trying not to wake him. He then slowly fondles him. Rocks is crying, as if feeling guilty for what he finds himself doing. Thabo wakes up.

THABO. Papa *he-e!* Papa *ntlogele!*[117] (*He cries again*) *O rile oka se tlhole o ntshwara gape . . . ntlogele* Papa . . .[118]

Rocks rapes the boy, speaking to him all the while.

ROCKS (*spiritually tortured*). Sorry, Big Boy . . . Sorry, my boy . . . *Skalla sani . . .* Papa *wa o rata, wa utlwa chana?*[119]

Blackout.

116 Lie down and sleep.

117 Papa, no! Papa, please leave me alone!

118 You said you wouldn't touch me again . . . leave me alone, Papa . . .

119 Don't cry, my son . . . Papa loves you, you hear *chana*?

Beat 7

A very drunk Dan and Lungi are going home, drunkenly singing a Zulu song, "Sandisa nge Cadillac."[120] *When they get to a certain point, they go their separate ways.*

LUNGI. Tomorrow, Dan!

DAN. Tomorrow! Remember, *no dice*—you go blind!

LUNGI. I'm drunk now—and you know drinking, it gives you the desire. I'd rather go blind! (*Walks off.*)

When Dan gets to his house, he finds a guy called Lovemore waiting for him.

DAN. And then?

LOVEMORE. Howzit, my friend?

DAN. What are you doing here?

LOVEMORE. You don't remember me? My name is—

DAN. I don't care what your name is. What I want to know is what you're doing in my house at this time of the night when I'm not here.

LOVEMORE. Look, I work with your wife. We've met before. My name is Lovemore Kata.

DAN. Motlholo . . . Dorah?! Dorah?! *Lekwerekwere le le batlang mo gaka bosigo jaana?!*[121]

LOVEMORE. No, no, no , no, my friend, don't call me a *Makwerekwere*. I'm a Malawian. I come from Malawi—I don't know a country called *Makwerekwere*.

DAN. What do you want here?!

LOVEMORE. I told you, I work with your wife!

DAN. This is not where she works, this is my house!

LOVEMORE. Wait a minute, my friend, I think you've had a bit too much to drink.

The furniture movers, Jabulani (30 years) and Buda (30 years), come through, carrying heavy household items.

---

120 *"We Flew in a Cadillac."*

121 What is this "*kwerekwere*" (derogatory name for a foreigner) doing in my house at this time of the night?

DAN. Hey, hey, wait a minute . . . What's going on here?

JABULANI. *Jonga la ndoda, asibizwanga huwe, asizanga kuwe! Siyeke sisebenze ndoda!*
He Buda, *mas'hambe!*[122]

DAN. *Haowa, madoda . . . madoda?*[123] (*They go out. Frustrated, Dan turns back*) *Mara*
go etsagalang ye?[124] (*Dorah comes through with her bags*) Dorah? What is this?
What's happening?

DORAH. I'm leaving you, Dan.

DAN. Lea . . . leaving me? Wha . . . what do you mean?

DORAH. This is Lovemore, I'm going to live with him from now on.

DAN. You're leaving me?! For a *kirigamba*[125] called Lovemore?!

LOVEMORE. Wait a minute with those names, my friend. I don't want to get
angry.

DAN. Get angry?! Get angry with who?! Get angry in my house?!

DORAH. Stay in your house, then. Come on, Lovemore, let's go.

DAN. Wait, wait, wait, Dorah, wait. Let's talk about this . . .

JABULANI. *Sisi? Sithatha konke mos?*[126]

DORAH. Yes, yes, all of it.

DAN. What?! (*They take the furniture. Dan stops them. To the movers*) *He lona, tloge-*
lang daai goetes, letla bona masepa![127]

DORAH. *Batlogele,* Dan, *ha osa batle ba ditseye ka fose!*[128]

He turns to Dorah. They exit with the furniture.

DAN. No, man! *Ema pele,*[129] Dorah. You can't take away the furniture . . . I con-
tributed a lot for buying these things.

DORAH. *E kebe ele kgale ba di tsere!*[130] They were once yours, now they're mine.
You only paid the deposit.

---

122 Look here, man, we were not called by you and we're not here for you! Leave us to
do our job. Hey Buda, let's go!

123 No, guys . . . guys?

124 What's going on here?

125 . . . foreigner . . .

126 My sister? Do we take everything?

127 Hey, hey, leave those things alone, if you don't want trouble.

DAN. *Mara* Dorah *o tsenwe ke eng ye?*[131]

DORAH. *O kolobe! Ke batla go go bontsha gore o kolobe . . . o kolobe* Dan, *ke batla go go tlogela ka yona hoko e ya gago*[132] . . .

DAN. *Mare*[133] Dorah why are you doing this to me? What have I ever done to you to deserve this?

Buda and Jabulani walk back in for more furniture.

DORAH. You broke your promise, Dan. You promised me *bliss*, you remember? *O ntshepisitse magodimo le mafatshe*,[134] but all I got was a limp dick.

Buda and Jabulani laugh.

BUDA (*as they pick up more furniture*). Limp dick—did you hear that?

DAN. What you're doing is wrong, baby. How can you talk like that to me in front of people? *O batla gore ba ntseye yang*[135] . . .

DORAH. It's the truth, Dan. You have nothing to offer except empty promises. Lovemore is more of a man than you'll ever be.

DAN. Yes, what do you expect, he's a *kirigamba*! These people use powerful herbs to enlarge their dicks! You can't compare me to *lekwerekwere*!

Lovemore grabs Dan angrily.

LOVEMORE. I will kill you, I will kill you, I will bash your face in!

DAN. Don't touch me, don't touch me!

DORAH. No, no, Lovemore, let him go. He's just a tired joke, you don't even need to do anything to him. Let him go.

Lovemore lets him go.

DAN. I'm not scared of you! I'm not scared of you! Come, come!

---

128 Leave them, Dan, if you don't want them to use force!

129 Wait a minute . . .

130 They could've long been repossessed!

131 Dorah, what's gotten into you?

132 You're a pig! I want to show you that you're a pig, I want to leave you in this pigsty of yours.

133 But . . .

134 You promised me the world and heavens, . . .

135 You'll make them disrespect me . . .

DORAH. Don't mind him, sweetheart. You have nothing to prove to him. You've already proven it to me—in bed, unlike him. Come on, let's go.

They take the bags and go.

DAN (*going after them*). Dorah? Dorah? Dorah? (*Crying*) Okay, go! Go, go, go! *O nagana gore ke tla go ncenga! Tsamaya* man! *Nka se go llele nie!*[136] And when things go bad for you, don't come back here, I won't be waiting! Go, go, go! (*He stops near the door and collapses to the ground, crying like a baby.*)

Buda and Jabulani come back for the last item, a table. Dan quickly rises and gets on top of the table as they try to take it.

BUDA. Hey, get off that table, *wena*, otherwise it's not only your dick that's going to be limping!

DAN. *O bua masepa, jou bleksem!*[137] (*He shouts out to the departed Dorah*) *Wa utlwa yanong* Dorah *gore o nthogisa ka di vuilpop!*[138]

BUDA. *Ke mang vuilpop wena?*[139] Get off the table!

JABULANI. Don't talk to him, Buda! . . . *Masi mthulule!*[140] (*Dan clings onto the table*) Tip him off, tip him off!

They tip him off the table and he falls hard onto the ground. He stays there. Buda and Jabulani exit. Dan rises slowly. In silence, he walks off, singing a Satchmo song: "Nobody Knows the Trouble I've Seen."

End of Act I

ACT II

Beat 1

Music. Dario is hitting a pregnant Matlakala. This is done all over the stage—it must look very cruel. The dialogue is improvised. Dario is saying very little. After a while,

---

136 You think I'm going to beg you! Go, man! I won't cry for you!

137 You talking shit, you rubbish!

138 Dorah, you see now that you're making this trash insult me!

139 Who is trash?

140 Get him off!

Dario freezes and Matlakala delivers a monologue to the audience.

MATLAKALA (*to the audience*). His balls had healed. He was out almost every night, fucking around. When I complained to him, he didn't listen. It was as if he didn't care. And because of that, I also started going out, hanging out with my friends and spent as little time as possible in my new home. He warned me about this, but I wasn't prepared to be the stupid housewife who stays at home, reading *Bona* magazines and gossiping about neighbors with other neighbors. So I went out with my friends. We went to parties, we went everywhere . . . I didn't care about my showing tummy, I just went everywhere and I had fun . . . And that's why he beat me up. He found me at my friend Patricia's house, and he beat me up all the way home . . . As if trying to embarrass me in front of people . . . (*Beat*) After beating me up like that, strangely, the baby survived . . . I resented that fact. I felt he had no right beating me up that way and still having his baby survive it. How could God be so cruel? How could God make him so happy? (*She removes the artificial belly. Music. The house has been set up by now and it is a mess . . . Matlakala sits down, crying for a while. She then stands up and starts cleaning up.*)

Her father walks in.

DAN. Matlakala?

MATLAKALA. Papa? What are you doing here?

DAN. I uh . . . I came to see you my baby.

MATLAKALA. Who told you where I was?

DAN. That friend of yours—what's her name? Patrick, or something . . .

MATLAKALA. Patricia?

DAN. Yes . . . Patricia . . . (*Attempting a joke*) Even though she's ugly enough to be a Patrick herself.

Matlakala smiles.

MATLAKALA. *Ei wena*,[141] Papa . . . I'm sorry, the house is a mess. (*She tries to tidy up.*)

DAN. You sound sick, what's wrong?

MATLAKALA. Nothing. I'll be fine.

DAN. I heard you were pregnant . . . You don't look pregnant.

---

141 Come on now, Papa . . .

142 . . . foreigner . . .

She sits on the couch, crying, all of a sudden.

MATLAKALA. I . . . I lost it. I lost the baby.

DAN. What? How?

MATLAKALA. He beats me . . . He sleeps around . . . He's never home, Papa . . . I killed the baby. My own baby. I killed her. I killed my own child just to get back at him. I . . . I killed her.

DAN. Ooh, my baby . . . What are you doing to yourself? Is this what you want? Look at you . . . just look at you. I mean, young as you are, living with a man under one roof? At your age? *He-e*, my baby . . . You're leaving with me, we're going home . . .

MATLAKALA. No, Papa, I can't. I can't leave . . . And besides, Mama doesn't want me back.

Beat. Dan turns pensive.

DAN. You mother is not home. You have nothing to worry about.

MATLAKALA. What?

DAN. Yes, she left me. Your mother left me for a *kirigamba*[142] from Malawi. After 15 years of marriage! Fifteen years!

MATLAKALA. Oh, I'm sorry, Papa.

DAN. It's okay, I'm a man. It's okay, I'll get back on my feet again, it's okay. (*Beat*) She even took my furniture with her. The house is empty now, I'm all alone there. I hear voices . . . I think I'm going mad . . . Please come back home, my baby . . . please . . . I miss you.

MATLAKALA. I can't.

DAN. Yes, you can. This is no life for you . . . I've stopped drinking, I'm busy looking for a job again . . . I'm trying to get my life into gear . . . Come and live with me.

MATLAKALA. Dario won't allow it, Papa. I've threatened to leave him before . . . he said he'd kill me. He's a dangerous man, he's a criminal. He hijacks cars, he kills people!

DAN. We'll go to the police. We'll make a plan . . . I'll protect you, my baby. I'll protect you. Please come with me.

DARIO. *En nou wena?*[143]

Dan is shocked to see Dario in actual person.

DAN. Hi, *bot*! Howzit?

DARIO. *Wat soek jy?!*[144]

DAN. Uhm . . . (*Laughing nervously*) It's a nice place that you have here.

DARIO. What do you want here?

DAN. Well, you see, *bot*, I'm . . . well, I'm Matlakala's father.

DARIO. *Eh monna, o batlang hie?!*[145]

DAN. I was just here to see how Matlakala is doing . . . Uhm . . . *Ja*.[146] But, it's okay . . . I'll . . . well, I'll come at another time.

He starts to go but Dario stops him. Dan is shit scared when he is stopped like this.

DARIO. Hey, hey, hey . . . Where do you think you're going? What're you doing in my house?

DAN. I was—I was—well, uhm, *bot* . . . you see, I was—I was just here to see . . . to see Matlakala . . . to see how she's keeping.

DARIO. *O kile wa mpona ke ile ko wena ke ilo cheka jou vrou?*[147]

DAN. Uhm . . . well, no. But, *bot*, you see . . . the thing is—

DARIO. What the fuck are you doing here then?

DAN. Okay, okay . . . you don't have to fight, *bot*. I was leav—

DARIO (*grabs him by the shirt*). Fight? Fight with who?

DAN. No, no, uhm . . . I'm sorry, *bot*. (*He lets him go.*)

DARIO. Listen here, *ne* . . . Go! *Vaya hie! Fela pleke!*[148] And if I ever catch you here again, I'm going to cut your dick off! *Verstaan my?*[149]

DAN. *Ja, ja*, sure. *Dankie bot!*[150] (*Rushes off.*)

Music.

---

143 And now?

144 What do you want?!

145 Hey man, what do you want here?!

146 . . . Yes.

147 Have you ever seen me at your house, visiting your wife?

148 Beat it! Get lost!

149 Understand me?

150 Yes, yes, sure. Thank you, brother!

Beat 2

The tavern is set up. Thuli is busy studying. After a while, Thabo walks in.

THABO. Hi.

THULI. We're not open yet.

THABO. What's that?

THULI. Who—I said, we're not open.

THABO. Physical Science? Is it hard?

THULI. Yes . . . uhm . . . actually, I don't know why I had to do it, I should've done History or—look . . . who are you?

THABO. I also used to hate it in high school, but now I'm obsessed with it. I can help you if you want.

THULI. Help me? Who are you?

THABO. I just want a drink. I wanted to sit and drink and read, but it's okay, I'll help you instead.

THULI. No, no, I'll be okay . . . We're not open yet.

THABO. Okay, I'll wait. What time do you open?

THULI. But you can't wait in here.

THABO. I won't be in your way. You can do your Science, I won't—(*Beat*) Where's your mother?

THULI. My mother?

THABO. Yes.

THULI. Do I know you?

THABO. Yes, you served me coffee the other day, and you told me that—

THULI. No one comes to a *shebeen* to drink coffee.

THABO. And I told you—

THULI. There's a first time for everything.

THABO. And then you said—

THULI. How do you read with so much noise?

THABO. And I said—

THULI. I hate silences.

THABO. And you said—

THULI. You're strange.

THABO. And I said—

THULI. I'm Thabo.

THABO. Yes, and that . . . you're beautiful.

THULI. I don't remember the beautiful part.

THABO. Well, *I* do . . . (*Beat*) You *are*, you know.

THULI. No, I'm not.

THABO. Okay then, you're ugly.

She laughs.

THULI. No, I'm not!

Just then, Mavarara walks in.

MAVARARA. Holla. (*No one replies. Kissing Thuli on the cheek*) Howzit, baby? *Ke vraza ho o bona?*[151]

THULI. I'm busy.

MAVARARA. What?

THULI. I'm busy.

MAVARARA. Ha man, don't be this way. I haven't seen you for over a month. Every time I want to see you, you tell me you're busy. What's up? *Keng okare wanxomela yana?*[152]

THULI. *Ke bizi!*[153] What must I do when I'm busy? I can't just leave my school work for you.

MAVARARA. *Ha wena okare wa jola wena!*[154] What? Have you found somebody else?

THABO (*to Thuli*). Look, I'll just wait over there, if you still want me to help you with your books.

---

151 Can I talk to you?

152 Why are you giving me the high hat (cold shoulder)?

153 I'm busy!

154 Why do I get a sense that you're seeing someone else?

MAVARARA. *Eintlek wena o mang?*[155]

THABO. *Nna?*

MAVARARA (*mimicking him*). *Nnywa?*[156] Yes, you! Who the fuck are you?!

THULI. Leave him alone.

MAVARARA. *Keng?*[157] Are you fucking her?! Is that why she's giving me the cold shoulder nowadays?

THULI. Just leave him alone. Why don't you just leave before I call my mother? . . . I told you I'm busy. Just—

MAVARARA (*taking out his gun*). *Voetsek! Tshek, sfebe!*[158] You think I'm scared of your mother? I'm sick and tired of this! *Hoe lank ke go jola o sa ntshe fokol?! Kante o twatwaziwa ke dinaai tsa di foureyes.*[159] I've been patient and patient, understanding when you told me you're not ready for sex yet. It's been too long now! Too long!

THABO. Leave her alone!

MAVARARA. *Fok jou, jou fokon gamors!*[160] (*He turns with the gun to Thabo and shoots. It is a spur-of-the-moment thing. Thabo is shot in the shoulder and falls to the floor. There is a moment of silence as Mavarara realizes what he has done. He turns to Thuli*) You see now what you made me do? Yeh? You see now?

All of a sudden, Thabo jumps at Mavarara from behind him and grabs him by the neck. Music. They struggle for a while for the gun. The gun goes off, but Thabo doesn't let go. He strangles Mavarara, who finally dies. Thabo moves away from him and sits on a chair, thoughtful. Thuli checks Mavarara's breathing. Music fades.

THULI. He's dead. (*She collapses beside Mavarara's body and sits in silence . . .*)

Thabo moves toward the audience.

THABO (*to the audience*). We didn't report it. We buried the body.

---

155 Actually, who the hell are you?

156 Me?

157 What?

158 Fuck you! Fuck you, bitch!

159 How long have I been seeing you without you putting out anything—only to find out that you're being fucked by this four-eyed idiot?

160 Fuck you, you fucking piece of shit!

She moves to him as she says—

THULI. It was all my idea.

THABO. No one reported him missing.

THULI. He was a criminal who lived alone. He was no longer in touch with his family back in Limpopo.

THABO. His friends assumed he had gone back to Limpopo and never bothered any more about him. It was a perfect killing. (*He holds Thuli in a loving manner*) From then on, Thuli and I, we shared a very deep, dark secret . . . It was a secret bond that would keep us together forever . . . Yes—we stayed together, even after what happened later.

They move off with the body as patrons pour into the shebeen. *Music.*

Beat 3

It is late at night. The patrons are at their tables in the shebeen. *Dan, very drunk, slowly gets on top of the table.*

DAN. People, lend me your ears . . . (*Lungi, who is seated drunkenly on one table, is alarmed when he notices what Dan is doing.*) If I was a white man, I would say "drinks for everybody on the house" like they do it in the movies . . . but— and a big BUT—I'm broke and blue . . . blue-and-broke. (*He laughs.*)

LUNGI. *Mgan' wam'*,[161] please get off the table!

DAN. *Bathong ke nale mathata.*[162] My life is nothing but hell.

LUNGI. Dan stop it, man! What is this? You're making yourself a laughing stock . . . If you're drunk, why don't you go home and sleep?

DAN. I have no home, *bot* . . . A home is not a home without a child or a wife. This is my home. Where's Mamiki? Mamiki?! *Okae*?![163] Mamiki?! (*Mamiki comes through again.*) Mami—(*Notices her*) Oh yes . . . I was just telling everybody . . . Your home is my home. This place is my home. The Spanish say, *Mikasa sukasa*: "my home is your home." But I don't have a home. So you should say that to me. Come on, say it . . . *Mikasa sukasa.*

---

161 My friend, . . .

162 People, I have problems.

163 Where?!

LUNGI. Dan, please man . . .

DAN. Lungi, you know my problems—

LUNGI. Dan, come down, please man. *Fuluga tafuli eo!*[164]

DAN (*laughs and mimicks Lungi*). "*Fuluga tafuli eo!*" Your Tswana is bad, my friend.

MAMIKI. Dan, *ake o fologe mowe tuu*! *Otlo nkobela di*-customer. I've heard enough *ke di* story *tsa gago. Ha re di*-social worker *rona . . . Fologa wa senya*![165]

DAN. Are going to give me one more round?

MAMIKI. If you don't get off there, I'm not going to bring it.

DAN. Okay, okay, my doll . . . Look, I'm getting off . . . (*He gets off the table. Mamiki disappears to the back. To Lungi*) Lulu?

LUNGI. Huh?

DAN. Lungeee? (*He gets off and plays around with Lungi by tickling him.*)

LUNGI. Stop it, man . . .

Dan has a moment with himself, as if a very depressing thought has hit him . . .

DAN (*introspectively*). *Goa nnyewa bot.*[166]

LUNGI. I don't understand you, *mgane wam'*[167] . . . I told you already, you have to deal with this boy . . . You can't get your wife back, but your daughter you can! All you have to do is what I told you. (*Tries to be discreet*) You have to take your life into your hands now . . . do something . . . deal with this boy. This boy can't treat you like this and you let him live. Besides, it's the only way to get your daughter back. Mhlaba is not a guy to be messed with. He never fails. Never! *Phela hi nkabi loya.*[168]

DAN. I don't have money to pay him, man.

LUNGI. I'll talk to him, don't worry. You'll pay him when you get a job.

Dan turns to the audience and addresses it.

---

164 Get off that table!

165 Dan, get off there, please. You're scaring my customers. I've heard enough of your stories. I'm not a social worker. Get off, you'll break my table!

166 Life is shit, my friend.

167 . . . my friend . . .

168 He's a Zulu hitman, that man.

DAN. Mhlaba was a Zulu guy from Natal. A very quiet loner Lungi had met in the *shebeen*. He was not a guy to be messed with. Rumor had it that he was an *inkabi*. *Inkabi* were Zulu hitmen who were famous for the many killings in the taxi industry. After Lungi talked to him about my situation . . . about that criminal boy Dario keeping my daughter as his prisoner, Mhlaba was more than happy to help . . . (*Music. We see the bleeding Dario crawling across the front of the stage, dying. He is followed by a serene,* panga-*wielding*[169] *Mhlaba. Dario dies slowly.*) He didn't waste any time in killing Dario. It was as if he enjoyed doing it. Dario's murder was never solved . . . Even those people that might have seen Mhlaba doing the killing never told the police what they saw. Lungi tells me it's because people like Mhlaba are deeply connected to their ancestors. I don't know about that . . . all I know is, I was happy to have my daughter back with me again.

Dan and Lungi walk out of the club. Mhlaba picks up the lifeless Dario and starts walking off stage with him on his shoulder.

Thabo and Thuli are at their table. They kiss like in black-and-white 1920s' movies. Just then, Mamiki comes in. She sees Thabo and Thuli kissing. She is outraged of course, shocked even.

MAMIKI. Thuli?! Thuli?! Thuli?!

THULI. Mama?

MAMIKI. How many times must I call you for you to hear me?

THULI. Sorry, *a ka go kwa.*[170]

MAMIKI. *O tla nkwa byang o nnetse banna.*[171]

THULI. *Ha ka nn—*[172]

MAMIKI. Shut up! There's school tomorrow, wash the dishes and go to sleep.

THULI. *Mare* Mama I'm talking to Thabo still. I'll wash them later—

MAMIKI. *Thuli, s'ka batla go ntena ntse ke tenegile, asemblief mosadi!*[173]

---

169 A variant of the machete, used in East and South Africa.

170 . . . I didn't hear you.

171 How can you hear me when you're focusing on men?

172 I'm not—

173 Thuli, don't piss me off when I'm already pissed off, please woman!

THULI. Bye . . . I'll see you tomorrow.

THABO. Sure.

Thuli leaves.

MAMIKI (*to Thabo*). Can I talk to you?

THABO. Sure . . .

MAMIKI. Not here. In my bedroom . . .

THABO. In your what?

MAMIKI. You heard me. (*She starts off and Thabo follows her.*)

Music for scene change. The bedroom is set up (but again such that we have both the shebeen area and Mamiki's bedroom on stage).

Beat 4

Mamiki and Thabo are in the bedroom area.

MAMIKI. What are you doing?

THABO. With what?

MAMIKI. My daughter . . . Thuli. What are you trying to do? (*He doesn't answer.*) We talked about this. Didn't I tell you about this? I asked you to stay away from her. Didn't I?

THABO. She's my girlfriend.

MAMIKI. What are you—what do you mean she's your girlfriend?

THABO. She's my girlfriend, I love her and she loves—

MAMIKI (*going berserk*). Shut up, shut up, just shut up! She can't—that's my daughter there! What are you talking about?

THABO. Look, I didn't want—

MAMIKI. Will you just shut up! I mean, you—listen here, what . . . what about, what about us?

THABO. Us?

MAMIKI. Yes!

THABO. There can't be "us" any more. I love her. I loved her even before we slept together . . . I loved her from the first time I saw her. It was . . . well, it was "love at first sight." Now she's my girlfriend . . . I love her and she loves me too, so you see . . . there can't be "us" any more, I can't do that to her.

MAMIKI. Don't come and tell me rubbish! You sleep with me and then you want to fuck my daughter?! Do you think I'm just going to say, "Go ahead, I give you my blessing?!" What game are you playing at? You can't fuck the both of us. I won't let it happen!

THABO. It's not like that, it's not like that! I don't just want to fuck her! Don't you understand? I love her! She means everything to me! More than you or anyone can ever mean to me! She makes me—every, everything that is bad in me, she turns to good . . . Do you know what I mean? Do you even know what that feels like?!

MAMIKI. I am taking this bitch away . . . I am taking her to her grandmother far, far away in the Limpopo where you won't find her.

THABO. I thought you said she means everything to you? And now you're calling her a bitch?

MAMIKI. Just get out of here, I don't even want to talk to you any more!

THABO. But—

MAMIKI. Just go! (*He starts off*) Thabo?! (*He stops. Tearful*) Wait! Please . . . don't go . . . I love you . . . Please, let's . . . let's just start from a clean slate and forget about all this . . . You stay away from Thuli and I will forget the whole thing ever happened. Just forget about her . . . Please . . . I know you're young . . . and she's also young, but . . . there's so many things I can give you that she won't be able to give you . . . I can give you anything you want . . . I have money . . . Huh? . . . I know it's not much, but it's enough . . . Just for the two of us . . . please . . . What do you say? (*She kisses him. He says nothing and he doesn't resist and doesn't fall into the kiss. Music. She kisses him again, this time more passionately. He plays into it after a while. She moves him to the bed, trying to take control like the last time, but all of a sudden he reverses the power play and he takes control. He becomes aggressive. Mamiki is impressed by this: she laughs with pleasure . . .*) Oooh, I like that!

He is now on top of her. He takes off her red G-string and continues to kiss her before he strangles her. After Mamiki dies, Thabo gets off the bed and as he tries to wrap the body with a sheet, Thuli enters. She is shocked at what she sees. There's a silent stand-off of horror between the two for a while. But as Thabo tries to explain to Thuli, reaching out to her, she runs off, screaming . . . He runs after her until he catches up with her in the shebeen *area . . . They fall over as he grabs her and in her hysteria . . .*

THABO. I had to do it. I had no choice. She was in the way, she was . . . she said she's going to take you away. (*Beat*) I can't . . . I can't lose you . . . You mean everything to me . . . When I'm with you, there's complete . . . peace within me . . . (*Beat*) You know, ever . . . ever since I started having this . . . this *urge* . . . to kill . . . to satisfy the raging nerves . . . I have always wanted that urge . . . that feeling to go away . . . But . . . I didn't know how . . . after meeting you, you made me feel good enough about myself for me to feel like stopping is . . . possible . . . Don't you see? . . . You're the air that I breathe . . .

He motions to kiss her, but she screams once again and runs off. He runs after her. Music for scene change.

Beat 5

We are now at Rocks Motshegare's house. Rocks arrives home from work. He is surprised to find Thabo in his house. He was already going for his gun.

ROCKS. Thabo? (*Thabo doesn't say a thing.*) Boy, can you run. My running is not what it used to be. I ran after you the other day, at the *shebeen*, but you'd disappeared into thin air . . . like a phantom. (*Beat*) Anyway, howzit Big Boy? (*Beat*) It's been a long time. Where have you been? Huh? No call, no nothing. I've been very worried. I looked for you everywhere. Jesus, just look at how you've grown. How long's it been?

THABO. Three years.

ROCKS. You speak. For a minute there I thought you had lost your voice. (*He laughs alone. Thabo doesn't find it funny. Rocks's smile fades*) Well . . . uhm . . . how . . . What do you do now? Did you . . . did you continue with your schooling?

THABO. I see the place still looks the same.

ROCKS. Yep.

THABO. And Mama's photos in the bedroom . . . they're still there.

ROCKS. Yep.

THABO. I thought you'd be married again by now.

ROCKS. No, no, I love your mother too much to do that. I wouldn't—look, Big Boy, you want coffee or anything?

THABO. I see her in my dreams, you know.

ROCKS. Huh?

THABO. And you too. The things you used to do to me, I have visions . . . terrible visions . . . The memories are strong.

ROCKS. Well, uhm . . . you know, it's good to see you again, "the Great." I can't begin to tell you how—

THABO. Do you hear me?

ROCKS. What?

THABO. I just told you . . . I have visions, vivid memories . . . of what you used to do to me.

ROCKS. Come on, *laaitie*,[174] man . . . the past is the past . . . It's not good to bring out skeletons from the past . . . I'm . . .

THABO. A changed man now?

ROCKS. Yes.

THABO. For you it's that easy, isn't it? Forget what you did to me. Just like that. As if—

ROCKS. Look, what do you want?

THABO. I want *you*! I want answers!

ROCKS. Well, I don't have answers, Big Boy! I know how you feel but . . .

THABO (*bursting out*). You don't know how I feel! You know NOTHING at all about how I feel!

ROCKS. Easy, easy, boy . . . lower your voice . . .

THABO. Why did you do it?!

ROCKS. Look, I don't want to go back there! You're my son and I love you but . . . if that's all you came to talk about then you should just go!

THABO. I'm not leaving until I get answers. Why did you do it?

ROCKS. Fuck off!

THABO. Why did you do it?!

ROCKS. I'm getting angry telling you the same thing many times, boy.

---

174 Equivalent of "child", "junior", "kid" and so on.

THABO. Why the fuck did you do it?! (*Rocks grabs Thabo in anger as if to crush him to pieces. Thabo produces a gun from under Rocks's chin. Rocks freezes. Thabo, calmly*) Move back! (*Rocks takes a step back.*) Again. (*Rocks moves back again.*) Take out your gun and throw it on the floor. (*Rocks goes for his gun.*) Slowly! Don't tempt me to shoot you. And I promise you, I will if you try any of your police tricks on me.

ROCKS. Easy, Big Boy . . . Look . . . easy does it . . . Don't get excited.

THABO. Take out your cuffs. (*He does.*) Throw them here. (*He does.*) Sit on the chair. (*He does. Thabo moves behind the chair.*) Give me your hands. (*Rocks does so and Thabo cuffs him.*) Okay . . . now that we're relaxed, let's—

ROCKS. This is too tight.

THABO. Shut uuup! (*Beat*) I need answers . . . Give me answers. Why did you do that to me? Huh? Why? Why did you do that?

ROCKS. Look, "the Great," uh . . .

THABO (*going beserk*). Just stop it with that "the Great" shit! Just fuck it! I need answers here! (*Drawling angrily*) I need you to give me answers! Clear and tacit answers, none of your bullshit!

ROCKS. I'm sorry, "the Great" . . .

THABO. Fuck sorry! Do you have any idea of the pain you caused me?! Huh?! Do you have any idea?!

ROCKS. Sorry, Big Boy . . .

THABO. I was young, man! I was fucking young! I was just a child! You don't do that to a child! I asked you and I asked you to stop but you still went on! You went on without listening! I'm fucked up now! If it was only a matter of a painful arse and a few piles now and then, I'd understand—maybe I'd've long forgotten! But you tore my soul apart! And now I can't deal with the memories, I can't deal with the demons that are in my heart! And to deal with them, I go and kill . . . I rape and kill people . . .

ROCKS. What are you telling me, Big Boy?! What do you mean?

THABO. I don't want to kill any more . . . I want to be normal like other people . . . (*He starts strangling his father*) I want to stop . . . I don't want to kill anyone any more . . . (*The lights change and Thabo's mother, Mihloti, appears . . .*) Mama?

MIHLOTI. Howzit, my baby?

THABO. I'm fine. I'm going to be fine. I'm going to be fine now.

MIHLOTI. I miss you, my baby.

THABO. I miss you too, Mama. Why did you have to die?! Why?!

MIHLOTI. That is not something you choose. It's something that just happens.

All this time Rocks is choking like crazy but Thabo obviously has practice in stran-
gling people—he is not even moving. He is crying and talking.

THABO. But why did it have to happen to you?! Why you?! Why not him?! Why
not him?! Why didn't he die in that car, Mama?!

MIHLOTI. It's no one's choice, my baby, it's something that just happens.

THABO. I love you, Mama.

MIHLOTI. I love you too, my baby. (*She walks off.*)

The lights change back. Rocks dies and stops kicking around.

THABO. I love you, Mama . . . I love you very much.

Thabo snaps out of his trance just as Molomo enters.

MOLOMO. Rocks?!

They both freeze . . . Molomo goes for his gun, but he clumsily lets it slip out of his
hands to the floor—because of his fear. Thabo goes for his own gun. Molomo tries
to run away but is shot before he can get anywhere. Thabo goes to him and checks
whether he is still alive. He shoots again. He then comes back to center stage and looks
at the audience . . . Just when they expect him to say something, the lights change for
the scene change . . .

Epilogue

The stage is now bare.

We continue with a sequence that resembles the one the story began with, but, instead of
Sibongile being the victim of the chase, it is Matlakala. This time we see the chaser—it
is Thabo. He chases Matlakala until he catches her. He rapes her and strangles her with
her G-string. When she is dead, he rises and addresses the audience. The sequence resem-
bles the opening scene exactly.

THABO. It's all just too fucking complicated. I didn't stop killing as I had
thought I would. I still had the urge, I still had the feelings, the demons

were still with me . . . I really did try to stop for a while but the feelings were just too strong. Now, I don't stress much about it . . . The way I look at it, it all depends on how you look at it . . . It's like the theory of relativity: "the appearance depends on where you're standing." From where *I'm* standing, this is necessary . . . It's all relative, really . . . I feel because I have a damaged soul, I am not wrong in doing this . . . The people that die, I no longer feel much for them . . . It's relative, I feel . . . If you look at it another way, through my eyes . . . these people are sacrifices to my demons . . . It's all like an indigenous African culture or society, where this tribe still sacrifice their virgins to the gods. The West may get outraged all it wants to, but the tribesmen will never see anything wrong with it because it is their culture. It is what they believe in . . . So you see, things are all relative . . . It all depends on how you look at it . . . It's all relative. (*He moves off.*)

A drunk Lungi and Dan pass drunkenly in the background. They stop for a while and both pee.

DAN. *Eish, bot,* you know my daughter is going to kill me when she sees me like this. I promised her I wouldn't touch the bottle again.

LUNGI. *I* didn't promise anything, nobody's going to kill *me.* But actually, I hate this veld, my friend . . . We'll get mugged to death here, let's go quickly.

DAN. I'm happy, *bot.* No one can kill me when I'm feeling like this. God is not that cruel. Why don't we both go to my place? I'm sure Matlakala has cooked one of those delicious recipes of hers.

LUNGI. *Eish,* thank you, my friend . . . And *mina,* I was going to eat a crust of dry brown bread before I sleep.

DAN. That's why it's great to have such a daughter, *bot,* come on.

They walk off singing drunkenly. The only light that remains on stage is the spotlight on the dead Matlakala. Blackout.

End of Play

FROM LEFT TO RIGHT: *Moagi Modise (Jan) and Lee-Ann Shepherd (Marietta Badenhorst).*
Photograph by Martin Koboekae.

BUSH TALE

MARTIN KOBOEKAE

FROM LEFT TO RIGHT: *Moagi Modise (Jan) and Lee-Ann Shepherd (Marietta Badenhorst).*
Photograph by Martin Koboekae.

Bush Tale was performed at Johannesburg in 2001 with the following cast.

JAN	Moagi Modise
MARIETTA	Lee-Ann Shepherd
DIRECTOR	Martin Koboekae

Scene 1

The stage resembles a veld. Withering bushes and shrubs give the impression that it has been a dry season. Wild grass grows in patches and is littered with dry leaves.

Suddenly the voice of a man fills the air. He sounds as if he is in pain or urging someone to perform better.

VOICE OF MAN (*shouting*). Push . . . push . . . push . . . push . . . (*A white woman of about 30 years runs onto the stage. She is gasping and seems to have been frightened by something. She runs around as if trying to find a place to hide. She hears the man's voice and stops to listen*) Push . . . push . . . push . . . black man! . . . Push!

The woman murmurs to herself and her eyes pop out.

WOMAN (*exclaims in shock*). Blacks!

She then rushes out the way she came in as if even more frightened.

A rusty wheelbarrow loaded with six bags full of mielies/corn *struggles on to the stage. The man's shouts of "push" can still be heard. The wheelbarrow is pushed by a black man who looks like a farm hand. He is dressed in overalls, black gumboots, and a skull cap. He pushes his load in and collapses next to it, panting heavily.*

MAN (*talking alone*). No more overloading. When God said a man should rest on the seventh day he didn't figure how tired I would be on this Thursday, *shu!* But no more overloading on this luckless wheelbarrow. It wouldn't matter whether it is the semi-blind Mamokobi or the wheelchair-bound Ramangole. When they say, "Put one more bag for me on your wheelbarrow," I will look you (wheelbarrow) in the face and I will say, "No more overloading." (*The woman comes rushing in again and startles the man. He jumps up*) Hey!

WOMAN. Hey you!

MAN. Madam!

WOMAN. You!

MAN. Yes!

WOMAN. Shh!

MAN. Shh!

WOMAN. You didn't see me.

MAN. I don't see you.

WOMAN. You didn't see me.

MAN. I didn't . . . (*They hear a twig snapping nearby. She quickly hides behind the wheelbarrow. Her hair is visible atop the load. Somewhat confused*) I can see you . . . but I didn't see you. (*More snapping of twigs. Closer now. She sinks further.*) I can't see you now. Whites! (*Pause*) When a man and a woman surprise each other, it is common for the man to say "Shh!" to a woman because he expects her to scream. Look, look, I don't feel threatened by you but you still said "Shh!" to me.

WOMAN (*sharply*). Shh!

MAN (*to himself*). I give up.

WOMAN (*whispers*). He is nearby.

MAN (*whispers back*). Who?

WOMAN. Him, the man . . . my man . . . my life.

MAN. All of that? With a combination like that, I fear you won't get far. Give up.

WOMAN. Not on my life.

MAN. Your life?

WOMAN (*jumping up suddenly, filled with terror*). Don't rape me. He will shoot you.

MAN (*looking in the distance and very relaxed*). He won't . . . he will simply crush my beautiful black bones to pieces. My poor bones. I don't mind him crushing my hip bone, it has always been a pain in the butt. (*Pats his hip and then his butt.*) Funny bedfellows.

WOMAN. Well, he is as strong as an ox.

MAN. He is a giant . . . these must be the broadest shoulders I have ever seen . . . he is not looking this way but I can imagine the face. It must be one of those faces that warn you that . . .

WOMAN. Do you see him?

MAN. I think it is him. This forest has no history of being inhabited by bears.

WOMAN. It is him, can I come out?

MAN. As long as your complexion is not going to reflect the sunlight, I think we should be fine.

WOMAN. That is racist.

MAN. I meant it as a compliment.

WOMAN. Yes, it is him. He is going to the truck.

MAN. It is easy to understand why you are running away from him. What is not easy to understand is what you were doing with him in the first place.

WOMAN. He is my husband.

MAN (*pretends to be shocked and sits on a rock nearby*). Now, why would you run away from your husband?

WOMAN. Who are you to ask me all this? My business is my business.

MAN (*smiles and extends his hand to her as if to share hers*). Madam, I am Jan. Pleased to meet you.

WOMAN (*looks at Jan's hand and then at his face. She prepares to leave*). I better be going. Thanks for not raising the alarm. Jan is a good name. Better than professor, advocate, doctor . . .

JAN. My people aspire to be professionals, Madam.

WOMAN. The name is Chelsea.

JAN (*laughs hard*). Chelseabun, Chelsea football club. (*Points at her*) Chelsea! Good English name.

WOMAN. In fact, Chelsea is my black name.

JAN. There is no Chelsea in all the African languages.

WOMAN. It is the name I use when I am in the company of black people. My real name is Marietta Badenhorst. But it has come to my attention that some black people mispronounce it and call me Marete, which I was told is a contemptible part of the male anatomy.

JAN. Quite contemptible when idle, but of course a respected part. The igniter of life. But it will be an insult to the male anatomy to call you by . . . (*she looks sharply at him*) . . . the other name. (*Noise of truck starting up and driving off.*) You have no wheels now.

MARIETTA. Where are you going, Jan?

JAN. You don't expect to get a ride on my wheelbarrow, and Jan is not my real name, it is my white name. My real name is Oven.

MARIETTA. Good name. Owen! But Owen is also a white name.

JAN. Oven.

MARIETTA. Oven?

JAN. You make it sound awful. But yes, I am Oven.

MARIETTA. Oven? As in micro-oven?

JAN. As in oven, for the stove.

MARIETTA. You are right. It is not a white name. Well, I better be going?

JAN. Where to?

MARIETTA. De Aar. Home.

JAN (*startled*). De Aar? Is that where you are coming from?

MARIETTA. That is where I am going.

JAN. But . . . is that your home town?

MARIETTA. Yes. That is my home.

JAN (*lets out a soft whistle, as if contemplating*). Well . . .

MARIETTA. You seem surprised.

JAN. I didn't know De Aar still exists. Maybe it is because nobody speaks about it lately.

MARIETTA. But even this place, what do you call it? Makwasie?

JAN. Leeudooringstaad.

MARIETTA. Well, if you can say Leeudooringstaad then my name is safe on your tongue. Okay, this Leeudooringstaad is never in the news, nobody speaks of it. Do you expect people to think that it is non-existent?

JAN. But De Aar was known for all the wrong reasons. I remember a white man who was hounded out of the town because he was living with a colored woman. The shop-owners served black customers through windows. A black guy could be charged for indecent assault by just looking at a white woman's dress hanging on a washing line. They had this rightists' movement which was hell-bent on destroying anything black. I just forget what they used to call themselves.

MARIETTA. Are you sure you are a farm laborer? (*Pats the bags and sits on them.*)

JAN. I am not, and I don't think the people who sent me to the mill with their corn will be amused to see you sitting on their food.

MARIETTA. They are not here.

JAN. One of them is a *sangoma* . . . you know . . . a bone-thrower.

MARIETTA. A witch-doctor!

JAN. He doesn't bewitch or put people under a spell. He is somebody who is able to tell accurately that some unidentified bum sat on the food of other people.

MARIETTA. Unidentified bum?

JAN. He won't be able to tell whose bum it was.

MARIETTA. Just now you were sitting on the bags.

JAN. He knows my bum . . . Badenhorst? Badenhorst was the leader of the vigilante group. Do you know him?

MARIETTA. Who are you to ask me all these questions? You are a stranger to me. I don't know you. Why should we be talking? We have nothing in common. You are a man, I am a woman. You are a farmhand or gardener, I am a teacher, you are black, I am white—we shouldn't be talking.

JAN. Well, I didn't go to De Aar to talk to you. This is my daily route to the mill. I have never seen you here before, but you came . . . (*From under the bags he takes out a small parcel and unwraps it. It is dried meat. He sits on the bags next to her and eats it. She opens her handbag and takes out a boiled cob of mealies.*) Dried meat.

MARIETTA. Corn.

JAN. It is like keeping a dolphin in a fish pond. Corn in a handbag.

She eats.

MARIETTA. I am sure the dried meat feels that it is in foreign hands.

JAN. Foreign but safe. And the corn must be itching to come this way.

MARIETTA. He is my father.

JAN. The corn?

MARIETTA. Badenhorst. The leader of that group.

JAN. If he finds us sitting here, he'll shoot both of us dead.

MARIETTA. He will shoot you. I am his daughter.

They eat.

JAN (*stands up and walks to the side and prepares to pass water against the trunk of a tree*). Fathers, daughters. That relationship is difficult to destroy. When daughters are getting married, mothers get excited because they want to get rid of the rascals. The protective fathers want to oppose but can't because they always remember . . . they too got married.

MARIETTA. Now, what do you think you are doing? You can't do that here.

JAN. Can't do what? I am doing nothing.

MARIETTA (*hesitates*). You can't pass water in the open like that.

JAN. Oh! You are talking about urinating. Come on, this is nothing.

MARIETTA. But you can't do that here.

JAN. Show me a toilet around here and I'll happily use it.

MARIETTA. It is indecent.

JAN. If you remove yourself from these serene surroundings, the indecency won't be so apparent. Like I said, this is my route and this is my routine.

MARIETTA. Besides, there is no water.

JAN. I don't intend to flush.

MARIETTA. To wash your hands. You are eating, you are licking your fingers, and one can't be sure that you didn't . . . do the same earlier.

JAN. Now you want to teach me basic hygiene. I wonder why, because every time you have looked at me you have seen filth, the downtrodden, stupidity, reckless sex, and a big penis.

MARIETTA. I have never seen you before, I have never seen your penis before (*Startled*) . . . God!

JAN. To you we are one and the same, yes, there is a natural link between filth and blackness. When your gardener-paraffin, or your messenger-advocate does something wrong, all black men are at fault.

MARIETTA. Those are politics and I don't wish to discuss politics. I just wanted to show you how indecent and unhygienic it is for . . .

JAN. . . . for me to hold my penis in my hand and take a decent pee, because my manhood is filthy?

MARIETTA. I keep on trying to stay away from politics and you keep on dragging politics into this.

JAN. So my penis is political?

MARIETTA. Jesus!

JAN. That is blasphemy . . . and I am sure your father didn't like to discuss politics as well.

MARIETTA. You leave my father out of this. I don't understand how an indiscretion on your part can take us to discuss my folks . . . it is just barbaric to pass water in front of a woman and it is just unhygienic not to wash your hands after that.

JAN. So you like me, Marietta?

MARIETTA. What?

JAN. You don't want me to eat with filthy hands, you care about me, you are worried about my digestive system, you are worried about me. It is good to know that you like me.

MARIETTA. Like you? . . . sies I don't like you. I can never like you.

JAN. My heart says I must like you, but my eyes say I must not, and I am sensible enough to listen to my eyes.

MARIETTA. Cheeky little bastard.

JAN. Aha! The Badenhorst blood is running thick now.

MARIETTA. I can report you to the police for your petulant behavior. I am full up to here with your incivility. My father is my father and I will not allow a pugnacious person like you to attack his dignity.

JAN. Dignity is diabolically hard to reclothe.

MARIETTA. Go away! Just leave! Go away!

JAN. Now angry too. Maybe you should leave. You found me lying here. You invaded my area and now you want me to leave . . . very reminiscent of our history. Twenty-first-century invader.

MARIETTA. I will leave. (*Prepares to go.*)

JAN. Marietta, I will leave.

MARIETTA. No, I will leave, I found you here. You are the boss here, because you go up and down, up and down with your wheelbarrow. So you think you own this area. I will leave.

JAN. I am a gentleman, I'll leave.

MARIETTA. I say you stay, I leave.

JAN. You are very bossy. But I am saying nothing about our history. (*He jerks the wheelbarrow and prepares to leave.*)

Just then they hear a twig snapping. Marietta takes cover behind the wheelbarrow while Jan runs around in bewilderment.

MARIETTA. . . . Do you think he has come back?

JAN. You are more familiar with his antics. If he has a history of pitching up unannounced and silently, then your terror is justified.

MARIETTA. Who said I am terrified?

JAN. What are you doing there? I don't see any open arms and seductive smile to embrace him. (*They hear footsteps*) I bet he is walking on his feet and hands. The steps are too rapid to be just one person.

MARIETTA. His shoes are big.

JAN. I didn't say the steps are heavy. I said they are too rapid. (*He investigates and comes back*) Two soldiers, and it looks like they are coming this way.

MARIETTA. Good.

JAN. Bad.

MARIETTA. What?

JAN. Well, bad for me. They will want to know what we are doing in the middle of nowhere . . . a black guy and a white woman so deep in the forest.

MARIETTA. I will explain.

JAN. They will not be amused. They will think you and I have been hitting the sack. (*Points at bags on the wheelbarrow.*)

MARIETTA. They know it can't be possible, unless you fancy the idea. They know you and I can't possibly have . . . They are not stupid.

JAN. These guys are geniuses. They can turn a molehill into a mountain. They did it with our schools—they turned them into battlefields. What about our churches which suddenly became political rallies? I am telling you, they come in here and take one look at us and your disheveled hair and they will just see Romeo and Juliet.

MARIETTA. What will they do?

JAN. They will inspect us.

MARIETTA. Inspect us for what?

JAN. For sex.

MARIETTA. What?

JAN. They will check my manhood right here and the doctor will check your thing at the hospital.

MARIETTA. That is obscene.

JAN. We are used to it.

MARIETTA. And don't ever mention my thing in public.

JAN. It is just the two of us . . . and I didn't mention it, I said "your thing."

MARIETTA. I'll hide again. (*Hides behind the wheelbarrow.*)

JAN. What about me, Marietta?

MARIETTA. You just play it cool. They will just pass by if they don't see me.

JAN. But they will think I have stolen the stuff. (*Indicates to wheelbarrow*) They will investigate and will see you.

MARIETTA. What can possibly make them think you stole the things?

JAN. I am black.

MARIETTA (*jumps up*). Okay, go hide yourself and I will let them see me.

JAN. Why?

MARIETTA. Because I am white.

JAN. But they will know you can't push the wheelbarrow.

MARIETTA. We both hide ourselves.

JAN. And the wheelbarrow?

MARIETTA. The wheelbarrow . . . we just leave it here. They won't bother, they know it is kaffir food. (*Jan looks intently at her and begins to whistle as if he doesn't care*) What is that?

JAN. "Weekend Special."

MARIETTA. I mean the whistling.

JAN. Yes, "Weekend Special," a very popular township song.

MARIETTA. But you will attract their attention.

JAN. It is deliberate. I want them to find this pure angelic white woman holed up in the middle of nowhere with this dark-skinned savage.

MARIETTA. Savage! It is a good name. It is better than Oven, more appropriate.

JAN. No. Kaffir is better.

MARIETTA. Kaffir? Why do you like politics so much?

JAN (*whispers urgently*). They are here.

She ducks. Voice from the side.

VOICE. Hey you! What are you doing there?

JAN (*with a smile*). Just on my way to the mill, boss.

VOICE. Haven't you seen a beautiful madam around here?

JAN. I have seen a madam, but I don't think it is the madam that my boss is looking for.

VOICE. Why?

JAN. The madam that I saw is not so beautiful. I can say . . . maybe plain.

VOICE. Is it?

JAN. Yes, my boss, not beautiful at all.

VOICE. Where did she go?

JAN. That way, my boss, she enquired about the way to Kimberley. She is apparently on the way to De Aar.

VOICE. My god! Did she speak with you?

JAN (*marveling*). Yes, my boss, she could not speak with the boss or any other white boss or madam. I was the only one around.

VOICE. Just remember one thing, man, all the madams are beautiful.

JAN (*nods*). All of them are beautiful, my boss.

Footsteps fade away. Marietta emerges and takes out a small mirror from the handbag and looks at herself for a long time.

MARIETTA (*grimaces*). Not so beautiful.

JAN. You are not Diana Ross.

He pushes the wheelbarrow and exits. She remains seated, looking at herself in the mirror.

Scene 2

Light fades in. Marietta is seated on a stump. She is uncomfortable. She stands up and walks behind the tree. Most of her body is concealed by the tree. Only her knees are visible. She is squatting in a position that suggests that she is relieving herself. Just then Jan pushes in his wheelbarrow with three bags on it. He sees her emerging from behind the tree.

JAN (*stops the wheelbarrow abruptly. Clearly surprised but looks the other way*). I thought it was very barbaric to relieve oneself in an area which lacks proper sanitation.

MARIETTA (*straightening up shyly*). You were not here. And it is uncivil to comment about matters pertaining to waste discharged from a female body, especially from the lower part of the body.

JAN. Your gentility is remarkable but my township brain stubbornly tells me that shit is shit, urine is urine, unless you want to be tedious and say "the excretory opening at the end of the alimentary canal." But you can become Dutch and say "hole."

MARIETTA. I am not Dutch.

JAN. Is hole what you normally say?

MARIETTA. I am a lady. I have been waiting.

JAN. Your ladyship made you wait?

MARIETTA. I am a lady, I can't say hole.

JAN. You have just said it.

MARIETTA. . . . . I have been waiting for you.

JAN. For me?

MARIETTA. I have been waiting for you because I wanted to get something straight. Your comment about my looks did not go down well with me.

JAN. You waited this long just for that?

MARIETTA. It means a lot to me. And I don't think you are qualified to objectively judge my looks. What is good for the black eye is not always good for the white eye. Your wife probably thinks you are handsome.

JAN. I don't have a wife.

MARIETTA. Your girlfriend.

JAN. I don't have a girlfriend.

MARIETTA. . . . Why?

JAN. It is none of your business.

MARIETTA. You are very ill-mannered. I am aware that the government is about to scrap the Immorality Act, and that they intend to open public amenities to all. Soon, you will be sitting next to me on a bus.

JAN (*Looks up the sky*). Thank God for the small mercies.

MARIETTA. You should be grateful to that, but for heaven's sake! You have no authority to address me like one of your concubines.

JAN. That is very abrasive.

MARIETTA. Your incessant discourtesy is baffling. (*She fiddles in her bag, takes out a cigarette and lights it.*)

JAN. I didn't know you smoked.

MARIETTA. You don't have to know.

JAN. Considering your tenacious propensity to observe basic hygiene, I find your smoking rather inconsistent with those principles.

MARIETTA. It is my life, you have yours. Everyone has his own life.

JAN. I suppose then everyone should live this life the way he deems fit. Freedom of choice.

MARIETTA. Politics.

JAN (*sits down*). Tell me, Marietta, why are white women given to this curious habit of smoking?

MARIETTA (*dismissive*). They can afford it. Now tell me . . . about my looks. Did you mean what you told that guy?

JAN. No, I didn't mean it.

MARIETTA. But you said it to him.

JAN. He made me say it.

MARIETTA. What?

JAN. He said all the madams are beautiful. Not all of them are beautiful. Somebody had to tell him that.

MARIETTA. So I am ugly?

JAN. Well, from a black perspective . . . Yes, you are not a beautiful person.

MARIETTA (*sits down wearily*). So to you I am ugly?

JAN. I guess people who call ugly "ugly" would be comfortable with that description.

MARIETTA. So what about the perspectives other than the black one? If there is a black perspective, then there certainly have to be other perspectives.

JAN. I know of black perspectives only. I am sure you have noticed that I am black.

MARIETTA. I notice that you are a communist and you don't even try to hide it.

JAN. Do you know Mother Teresa?

MARIETTA. I am better learned than you. I am supposed to know that. She frolics in India and cuddles hapless children in impoverished Third World countries and she has only one dress.

JAN. She is one of the most beautiful people to have ever inhabited this planet.

MARIETTA. I have never seen her picture when she was young.

JAN. She is still beautiful. Even more beautiful than when she was young.

MARIETTA. With all the wrinkles and frailty?

JAN. Decrepitude and all. Everyone has the potential to be beautiful. If you want to be beautiful, you can, without plastic surgery. That is purely extraneous. What we need is inner beauty.

MARIETTA. Don't be judgmental and self-righteous. We all behold beauty in the same way beauty pageants behold it. Smooth skin, make-up, nice figure, and a beautiful costume. Well, you won't know anything about beauty pageants.

JAN (*laughs*). I was once a judge at a very prestigious beauty pageant.

MARIETTA. You? With all your Mother Teresa as a benchmark? I am sure you couldn't find a winner.

JAN. Somebody won.

MARIETTA. If the audience didn't kill her, she probably ended up in a zoo.

JAN. You are very concerned about looks.

MARIETTA. All women are.

JAN. Not all women that I know place too much credit on the beauty of the body.

MARIETTA. Next time I say all women, you must know I am talking about white women.

JAN. I'll try to remember that.

MARIETTA. In all my life, I have never had a man say I am ugly.

JAN. That species is never to be trusted with the truth.

MARIETTA. It is like any positive thing about my looks makes you unhappy. Why do you rejoice in my humiliation?

JAN. It shouldn't bother you. I am black. (*He takes out a flask of water from between the bags on the wheelbarrow and drinks.*) Not so cool. (*He replaces it.*) It is getting late, Marietta, I'd better be going. Your lifts home are also going to be scarce later.

MARIETTA. I will go by train.

JAN. Well, you have ample time. The train leaves at five. If you walk to the station now, you should be there within 30 minutes. Up there, you can see it from here. It will give you two hours' rest. Bye. (*Pushes wheelbarrow away.*)

MARIETTA (*runs after Jan*). Wait, my husband . . . when you saw him earlier, you commented about his looks. Your comment was not too complimentary. You said he looked like a bear.

JAN. Bears are cute. That is why girls fall all over themselves to get them.

MARIETTA. But you also said you didn't know what I was doing with him in the first place.

JAN. I was merely thinking about physical compatibility.

MARIETTA. Sex?

JAN. You are Dutch. But yes, sex.

MARIETTA. Your rampant testosterone makes you lose sight of your place now. How dare you think about me along those lines? How do you get it right to conceive such thoughts in your mind. The only thing that stops me from considering suing you is because you won't be able to pay (*pause*) and what exactly were you thinking? That you could have sex with me?

JAN. That your bum seems a bit too narrow for him. (*She slaps him hard. Rubbing the struck cheek*) We are square now . . . I am the first man to say you are . . . not beautiful and you are the first woman to slap me.

MARIETTA. I'll put you in your place.

JAN. You are intolerantly authoritative.

She takes out a cigarette and tries to light it but fails. He uses his lighter to help her.

MARIETTA. Do you smoke?

JAN. I also carry a knife but I don't go around stabbing people.

MARIETTA. A simple no would have done the trick.

JAN. So when your husband returns . . . sorry, it is none of my business.

MARIETTA. He is not my husband.

JAN. You should run for political office. You will be useful in the Ministry of Information. You really know how to confuse.

MARIETTA. I am not a liar. I am not married. He is a family friend whom my father holds in high esteem. Unfortunately, I don't share the same opinion. We are on our way to . . . he is on his way to the nudist colony. Of course, you won't know what that is.

JAN. The Beau Brummel Nudist Colony.

MARIETTA. You surprise me. Well, yes, that one, there is a protest tomorrow. The patrons think that because public amenities will be opened to all, the colony will also be affected. It is quite an affront to see a group of white people in their birthday suits but quite hellish to see a group of blacks naked.

JAN. Oh! White people will be in their birthday suits while blacks will be naked.

MARIETTA. Politics, Jan, politics.

JAN. Maybe white men are scared of being outgunned by their black counterparts.

MARIETTA. Is it true?

JAN. I don't know, you have to ask white men, I said maybe, I am not sure.

MARIETTA (*hesitating, almost blushing*). I mean the size.

JAN. You better decide for yourself. (*Approaches her and pretends to drops his pants.*)

MARIETTA (*runs away from him*). No! Don't! Are you silly?

JAN (*smiles*). I just wanted to show you the facts of life.

MARIETTA. That is public indecency.

JAN. It is just the two of us here.

MARIETTA. You keep on saying "it is just the two of us here." What are you up to?

JAN. But you keep on saying "public, public" as if there are other people around here. (*Pause*) He must be very brave.

MARIETTA. Who?

JAN. Your husband . . . your family friend. He deserves the presidential bravery award. To go naked in a body like that takes great courage.

MARIETTA. What will it take to improve your manners? Your insolence reflects the way you were brought up. You show no respect to women, you show no respect to white people. Jesus! Take your bitterness somewhere.

JAN. I am not Jesus.

MARIETTA. Damn blasphemous monster. Full of profanity.

JAN. The only profanity I know is of people uncovering their bum and farting in the face of God and justice.

MARIETTA. Don't you raise your voice at me!

JAN. Don't you point your finger at me!

MARIETTA. Go away! What are you doing here?

JAN. I am working. I am taking a break from my work, but it seems I need another break from you. You should have gone to the station earlier, but you don't want to go there, you want to stick around with me, you want to hang around with me, you want to be with me, you even wait for me.

MARIETTA. Wait for you? Stick with you? Why would I want to stick around with you? You don't amuse me.

JAN. I fascinate you.

MARIETTA. Fascinate's ass. (*Quickly slaps herself in self-reprimand. Jan looks at her in amazement*) I don't normally use that kind of language. I only use it when in a distressing situation.

JAN. And I am the harbinger of that distressing situation?

MARIETTA. You are that situation.

JAN. Thank you.

MARIETTA. Fuck you.

JAN. I am elated.

MARIETTA. You are full of shit.

JAN. It is pleasing to note that you realize that. (*Handles the wheelbarrow and prepares to leave.*)

MARIETTA. I am trying to hate you.

JAN. You fail. (*Exits.*)

Marietta is stupefied. Lights fade out.

Scene 3

Same setting as the previous scene. Marietta is pacing up and down the stage. Jan is heard approaching with his wheelbarrow. He is singing a folksong. He stops singing and heaves heavily. Marietta sits down.

JAN. Push . . . push . . . black man . . . push . . . Scumbag . . . push . . . lazyman . . . Push damn it. (*He pushes the wheelbarrow laden with bags onto the stage. He sees Marietta.*) Why am I not surprised to see you here?

MARIETTA. Maybe you are incapable of being surprised.

JAN. It is like I was expecting to find you here.

MARIETTA. I didn't wait for you. I can't wait for you all night. I was late for the train.

JAN. Late for the train? You had more than two hours to catch the train.

MARIETTA. When the train left, I was in the Ladies room.

JAN. Toilet. Where were you when it arrived?

MARIETTA. In the toilet . . . I am sure.

JAN. You are sure?

MARIETTA. I think so. When I came out of the toilet, they said the train was gone.

JAN. It was a long session.

MARIETTA. What? What are you getting at? Are you counting the minutes I spent in the toilet or are you insinuating that I deliberately missed my train? I was late.

JAN (*laughs*). Oh yes, the train left without you. How could I miss to notice that?

MARIETTA. Here is my ticket, you idiot. (*She takes the ticket out of the bag and pushes it in his face.*) Check it.

JAN. I am not a ticket examiner.

MARIETTA (*looks intently at him*). Jeepers! You look uglier than yesterday.

JAN. It pleases my heart. And you look better today. It is just that your mouth is a bit too big for any claim at genuine beauty.

MARIETTA. Do I talk too much?

JAN. That as well, but I was referring to the size.

MARIETTA. It pleases my heart.

JAN. What are you up to? That is my line.

MARIETTA. But not your property. Tell me, don't you get tired of traveling the same route every day . . . the rickety wheelbarrow . . . the bags of corn . . . your resting place here and so on? Don't you feel like being someone else or doing something else?

JAN. This is a situation which I have accepted. Like you have accepted your whiteness and femininity, I have also accepted my fate.

MARIETTA. But I have no problem with my whiteness and femininity and I can do nothing about that.

JAN. How can I be someone else like you suggest I should?

MARIETTA. I was not talking about physical transformation. I was merely referring to conditions which make you a better person. Like becoming a teacher or something.

JAN. If my work is routine, so is teaching. But I must point out at times I wish I were God.

MARIETTA. *Shu!* That is a big one, it is like an atomic bomb. Why would you wish for the impossible?

JAN. Precisely for that. I cannot achieve it.

MARIETTA. Stop wishing, then. But say your wish was granted and you were God.

JAN. That will make me very unpopular with you.

MARIETTA. You have never been popular with me.

JAN. Let me see.

MARIETTA. I know you were going to exterminate us all.

JAN. Exterminate who?

MARIETTA. Us whites.

JAN. It wouldn't be necessary . . . I would not have created you in the first place.

MARIETTA. That is diabolic.

JAN. The devil is black. Just joking. I would have created you. I would have created everything the way it is. The only difference would be that the black man would be boss and the white man, servant.

MARIETTA. And that would mean?

JAN. That would mean your last sentence would have ended with "my boss."

MARIETTA. That will be the day.

JAN. My wife will be "Madam" to you.

MARIETTA (*playfully*). And I will be cleaning your house, shining your stoep,[1] doing your washing and ironing for you.

JAN (*playfully too*). The ironing will be minimal. Wash-and-wear will be my speciality. And the wardrobe will consist of six identical khaki shorts, six pairs of rugby socks, two pairs of steel-toe brown boots, and a green crimplene suit with a pair of grey shoes.

MARIETTA (*to herself*). Madam?

JAN. Not me, my wife.

MARIETTA. But you said you are not married.

JAN. But the boss must get a madam.

MARIETTA. Your wish is becoming too adventurous now. God normally listens to irrational wishes, but I am sure she will be upset with your wishes' foray into the unthinkable.

JAN. She? Did you refer to God as she?

MARIETTA. God is a woman . . . has to be a woman. Why the espousal of love if God was not a woman? Love is something foreign in the daily activities of men. Look at yourselves. Beard, your physique all roughed up and not well proportioned, the war . . . who causes them? The destruction, the habitual untidiness and, to cap it all, your external reproductive organs look vile, and when you want to make love they look vicious, like you are going to war.

JAN. Sex is war. Hard! Rough! Sweat!

MARIETTA. Is that how you make it?

JAN. It is beastly to have all those elements present at the same time, but yes, they do occur, at times two at a time. And you can't reach 25 without having gone through all of them.

MARIETTA. I haven't.

JAN. Well . . . in the army there is something called slow march. And, Marietta, if God was a woman, don't you think your clitoris would be 10 times bigger than it is now?

---

1 Terraced porch in front of a house; verandah.

She slaps him hard.

MARIETTA. You dirty rascal! How dare you speak of me like that?

JAN. Thank God Almighty you are not a woman. (*Looks at her*) She would have given you more strength . . . so much for men going to war.

MARIETTA. I act on your provocation.

JAN. I am beginning to know.

MARIETTA. You'll learn.

JAN. I don't have a third cheek.

MARIETTA. You have a groin.

JAN. There are still many wars to fight. (*Pushes the wheelbarrow toward the exit; places himself between her and the wheelbarrow*) Marietta, did you know that the clitoris is the only human body part which has no other function but to give sexual pleasure only?

MARIETTA (*flashes a cigarette*). You are having an unhealthy obsession with sexual matters. Give me a light.

JAN. No. I am not dumb. Do you want me to lay myself bare to your incursions?

MARIETTA (*puts the cigarette away*). You seem well-versed on issues pertaining to the female body.

JAN. Black female body. But I guess you are the same. At least, in many respects. (*He drinks water from his flask and puts it away.*)

MARIETTA. Not exactly the same. It is like your corn and cornmeal. You can boil your corn and eat it. Or you can take it to the mill and grind it so that you can have cornmeal. Which do you like? Boiled corn or cornmeal?

JAN. I like them both. Maybe I eat more cornmeal than boiled corn, but, pardon my ignorance, what is your point?

MARIETTA. Your statement about women being the same. I am responding to that. Women originate from the same source, but are forced to undergo transformations by institutions like the school, church, and yourself.

JAN. Me? I have never played any active role in your life, I am black. But that is typical, every time something goes wrong, it is the black man. My mother once said to me, "My son, go out and do your best. But don't forget, your head will always be full of shit. But don't worry, it won't be your fault; the white man will always mistake your head for a toilet seat."

MARIETTA. I have seen better heads sitting on yours! Well, my mother warned me by saying, "My girl, your husband is never to be trusted too far and a black man is never to be trusted too near. If you have to give him something, put it on the ground and leave."

JAN. Your mother must have been a firebrand. I am sure you two got on well together.

MARIETTA. She inspired me on many things, but we eventually drifted apart. She was too methodical for my liking and the other thing that irritated me was that every time I did her a favor, instead of thanking me she would thank God.

JAN. What bothered you then? You and God are from the same stable, the only thing is that God doesn't go around beating people up.

MARIETTA. A simple and direct acknowledgment to the doer can be very gratifying. God is very fair and rational. She wouldn't take accolades that are not rightfully hers.

JAN. Hers? What color is God?

MARIETTA. God has no color, her being transcends colors.

JAN. I see. God has gender but no colour. That is curious, but undemonstrable. If that could be converted into an intelligible language, I would say it would be a source from which we should all quench our thirst for enlightenment.

MARIETTA. . . . . I am thirsty.

JAN. The water is a mile away.

MARIETTA. What have you been drinking?

JAN. Water.

MARIETTA. Let me have some.

JAN. Eh, um, it is black water.

MARIETTA. What?

JAN. I have been drinking directly from the bottle.

MARIETTA (*as if to herself*). Black water? Clear, pure, colorless, that is water. Clear, pure, colorless, that is God. You say your water is black. I am sure you will want me to believe that God is also black.

JAN. God can't be black. He would have played a more significant role in my life.

MARIETTA. You don't believe in God, the way you talk, it is like you never pray to him.

JAN. You said "him?"

MARIETTA. I am using your perspective. You used mine earlier.

JAN. I used to pray . . . a lot, but God doesn't seem to be interested in my affairs. And I said, the water is black because I drank directly from the bottle and you being white can't drink from the same bottle from which a black person drank. It must be one of the things your mother inspired you on.

MARIETTA. Let me have some water.

JAN. No.

MARIETTA. I am thirsty,

JAN. I can run and get you bottled water from the station cafe.

MARIETTA. I am dying of thirst.

JAN. I am a fast runner.

MARIETTA. What is the issue here? Don't you want to drink from the same bottle with me? You can throw it away after I have drunk.

JAN. I bought it.

MARIETTA. So that is it then. You cannot share with me.

JAN. No! I mean I wouldn't throw the bottle away, under no circumstance. I bought it, and you are so white. (*Marietta approaches and he retreats. She takes out the bottle, opens it and drinks. She puts it back.*) I am stunned, but the skies didn't crash down . . . for now at least.

MARIETTA. Who are you Jan?

JAN. *Ofentse*.

MARIETTA. *Oventse?*

JAN. *Ofentse* . . . which means the one who is victorious. The white clerk who worked for the Birth Registry Office couldn't write *Ofentse*, my mother could not spell it for for him, so he registered me Ovens. It is cumbersome to carry the name of a compartment of a stove but quite stressful to be called by more than one of those. So Ovens became Oven.

MARIETTA. Quite a history.

JAN. Quite a history. I have to go now. I promised the people I would be early today. The other lady has nothing to feed the kids when they return from school. I promised that I would be back before school is out.

MARIETTA. When will I see you again?

JAN. I don't know. When will you be on your way to the nudist colony again?

MARIETTA. I don't think I will.

JAN (*pushes the wheelbarrow toward the exit*). Oh! I nearly forgot. (*Takes out a packet of cigarettes and extends it to her.*)

MARIETTA (*amazed*). How did you know you would find me here?

JAN. I told you I was not surprised to see you here . . . actually, I went to the station and I saw you deliberately missing your train. I just sat there watching you till late. When that porter scolded that elderly couple alighting from the train, I saw you intervene and heard you publicly castigating him for his belligerent behavior.

I heard you tell him not to make the station be known for all the wrong reasons. I knew you were quoting me on the De Aar statement and I knew I had made an impression on you. You defended the frail and helpless who happened to have the wrong color. It was the first time in all my life that I heard a white person reprimanding another white person in front of black people. Well?

MARIETTA (*takes cigarettes from him*). You even got the blend right.

JAN (*laughs*). I am a dunderhead who can remember.

MARIETTA. Stop it now. Yes, I tried hard to hate you. Yesterday I waited for you, not because you said I was ugly, but because I wanted to interrogate my feelings. I didn't want to go home with excruciating thoughts and feelings. I waited because I wanted you to behave in a manner that is consistent with my expectations of you.

JAN. And?

MARIETTA. I was disappointed.

JAN. But I have been trying my best to behave since you have begun to frequent this place.

MARIETTA. Frequent? You cannot justify that.

JAN. For one and a quarter days, it is more than enough.

MARIETTA. I see I am not welcome here.

JAN. You are, and when you drank my water, something yelled inside me and said "Oh yes!" I think it was my late father.

MARIETTA. I hope we are not going to touch on superstitions now. I am a person of logic . . . I am a teacher, you know.

JAN. We both are.

MARIETTA. What?

JAN. We are both teachers.

MARIETTA. You! A teacher?

JAN. Yes, it is just that I am not teaching at the moment. I was suspended for my beliefs.

MARIETTA. Politics? . . . well, it has to be.

JAN. It has to be. But it seems the suspension has turned into a dismissal now. They don't want to lift it. I intend to challenge the authorities in court.

MARIETTA. At least, there is a commonality.

JAN. Are you also taking them to court?

MARIETTA. No, but we are both teachers.

JAN. One is inside and the other outside. In limbo. (*Pause*) You are beautiful.

MARIETTA (*frowns*). Like Mother Teresa?

JAN (*laughs*). Like yourself.

MARIETTA. You flatter me. And my mouth?

JAN. Fits perfectly. I wonder why I didn't notice that earlier. Maybe it is because you speak too much.

MARIETTA. Really?

JAN. Maybe I tried too much to see evil in you.

MARIETTA. You failed.

JAN. That's my line.

MARIETTA. You have no exclusive rights to it. What do we do now?

JAN. You are white, I take advice from you.

MARIETTA (*shakes her head*). Your turn to take responsibility.

JAN. I have been responsible all my life. I have supported my mother and son.

MARIETTA. A son? But you said you are not married.

JAN. Black people love babies, married or not.

MARIETTA. That's funny.

JAN. That's sad. Love can't feed them.

MARIETTA. I have asked a question.

JAN. About what?

MARIETTA. You can't pretend not to see what is happening.

JAN. I don't see it.

MARIETTA. You don't?

JAN. I feel it.

MARIETTA. And?

JAN. It is dangerous. It scares me.

MARIETTA. Are you scared to fall in love with me?

JAN. We will land in trouble.

MARIETTA. You don't look like a coward.

JAN. I am claustrophobic. Jail will kill me.

MARIETTA. What do you suggest we do?

JAN. I only know what I will do, and that is to keep on pushing this wheelbarrow daily and try to forget that I met you.

MARIETTA. Will you succeed in doing that?

JAN. I will. I have succeeded in forgetting that I am a man born with dignity.

MARIETTA. You are giving up.

JAN. I am following common sense and safety.

MARIETTA. I know that kind of common sense, and it truly is common.

JAN. Go back to De Aar, Marietta. Teach the little ones about love and forgiveness and you will forget about your trip to the nudist colony.

I really would love to see a colony of white people naked. I have got high expectations.

MARIETTA. High expectations? You may be very disappointed. (*Walks away from him, takes out a cigarette*) Have you got a light for me?

He takes out a lighter, walks toward her and lights for her as the lights fade.

End of Play

Fats Bookholane (Menzi). Photograph by Ruphin Coudzer.

HALLELUJAH!

XOLI NORMAN

Lerato Thooe (Lady). Photograph by Ruphin Coudzer.

Hallelujah! was performed at The Barney Simon Theatre at the Market Theatre Complex until August 26, 2001.

LADY	Lerato Thue
BONGA	Oscar Motsikoe
MENZI	Fats Bokholoane
DIRECTOR	Fiona Ramsey
MUSIC DIRECTOR	Xoli Norman

Scene 1

In the dark, we hear the sound of a ringing cellphone. As the lights come up, we see a sparsely furnished living room with a Victorian sofa behind which is a window. There is a kitsch picture of a bleeding Christ on the cross hanging on the wall. Not far from it is a picture of Miles Davis. There is a door leading to the bedroom. Bonga is sitting on the sofa, making notes in a notebook. Lady answers the phone.

LADY. Hello . . . Yes . . . Please hold . . . (*To Bonga*) It's yours.

BONGA. Hello . . . Yes, Mr. Jones . . . Fine how are you? Tough, but what can we say, these are those—"best of times worst of times kind of times" ha, ha, ha, ha, ha. So, what is not happening?—talk to me Mr. Jones.

JONES. As you know, Bonga, times are bad . . .

BONGA. No, that is true . . .

JONES. It can't happen, man, it's just that . . .

BONGA. What do you mean? (*Lady is leaning against the door, listening to Bonga who is speaking agitatedly on the cellphone*) That was the agreement, Mr. Jones. . . yes . . . NO . . . You guys are going back on your word! What do you mean? Of course, yes . . . That is what I was told . . . you personally told me categorically that . . . No, what about you listening to me?! It's the whole fuckin' smokescreen bullshit game again. I wish I had listened to Menzi. The people know about your dirty tricks, it won't be long before they burn your house down, you wait and see. I want my fuckin' manuscript!

JONES. I think you are overreacting here, Bonga.

BONGA. I don't care!

JONES. All I am saying is . . .

BONGA. You just give me back my work!

There is grave silence. Bonga sits on the armrest of the sofa.

LADY. Bonga, that is no way to talk to people.

BONGA. Oh, there you go again. It's always me. (*Lady advances and sits on the sofa.*) What about what they are doing to me? No, I'm too minute an element in the big scheme of things. I don't count. Let me tell you something, Lady—I work hard. I don't expect miracles. I work hard and I expect the same respect I put into my work. I . . . SHIT!

LADY. Even if you work hard, Bonga, that does not justify the way you just spoke to the person on the phone.

BONGA. What was I supposed to say? They are the ones that stopped me from talking to other publishers, made me believe they would stand by their word—"Mr. Miya we really love your work, we are very much interested in being the first ones to publish you."

LADY. Did they really say that?

BONGA. Of course, they did! Do you think I'm just raving out of madness?

LADY. Give me that phone. (*She leans over and gets the phone, punches numbers and paces while she waits.*) This is Lady . . . No, I don't think that will be necessary. I have two things to say to you, Mr. Jones. One—Bonga is a very special man in my life, if that means anything to you at all. Two—it took Bonga a lot of effort and time to put art to paper and your call ruined it all. You think because you flaunt huge monies, you can make and break people's lives with a snap of your fingers? Well, take this and put it in your pipe— people are people and they matter more than all the monies of a million publishers—I hope you enjoy the smoke.

JONES. I think you are taking things out of context here, Mrs. Miya.

LADY. No I am not taking things out of context. You personally promised to publish his poetry! (*Ends the call, and throws herself on the sofa*) Nani kodwa Bonga *niyahlupha*.[1] You write such big words and yet can't do a simple thing like put their words to paper, insist on a written contract.

BONGA. I took his words in good faith.

LADY. Well, I hope you've learnt your lesson—promises for writers must be written down. (*There is silence as she looks at him with compassion.*) What happened to the other publishers? The first ones you took your work to?

BONGA. Ikusasa Lesizwe?

LADY. *Ja*. What happened to them?

BONGA. *Ag* them, I asked Bro Menzi to put in a good word for me.

---

1 You upset me just as well, Bonga.

LADY. And?

BONGA. I'm still waiting. Menzi says I breathe hope and death in the same breath—I don't know what he means by that.

She looks at his crestfallen face.

LADY. What are you going to do now?

BONGA. Give me 50, I'll go and see Bro Menzi.

LADY. The bar again? Why don't we visit Bafana and Nomsa?

BONGA. No, I'm going to see Bro Menzi.

LADY. Bongs dear, how long has it been since we spent time with them?

BONGA. You were with them just yesterday, Lady.

LADY. I mean us, together as family. Visiting them together. (*As she exits*) Sometimes I just wish you could grant my wishes. (*Exit.*)

She re-enters with her purse in hand, takes out a few notes and gives them to him. Bonga is overcome with affection as he looks at her. He doesn't take the money.

BONGA. Come, let's go visit Bafana and Nomsa.

Lady gets very excited at the suggestion. She hugs and kisses him.

Scene 2

Jazz bar. Menzi is about to render a poem on the bandstand as the the jazz tune "The Poet" plays.

MENZI. Wish I could dance like a poet
    Waltz on one leg across the paper's cape
    Leaving immortal stains with each twist
    And muted words that echo eternally . . .
    (*Gives the pianist a discontented look*) What key are you playing in?

PIANIST. Key G, Bro Menzi.

MENZI. Then don't play—F sharp, half-diminished.

SAX. But the progression leads to F sharp half-diminished in the 6th bar.

MENZI. It doesn't sound good, try a D 7th or any mode within that whole tone scale.

SAX. But that is going to sound odd—the diminished chord gives the tune a different color, Bro Menzi.

MENZI. It makes it sound too melancholic. The tune must support the poem, make it a bit light.

SAX. But the song is not written like that, Bro Menzi.

BASS (*getting a glass of water from the bar*). Kaya, come on, man! Just play this shit the way Bro Menzi wants it. Finish and *klaar!*[2]

Kaya gives the bass player a hard look.

KAYA. *Ukhulumani manje wena?*[3] I am the bandleader here.

MENZI. And this is my gig. (*Kaya starts packing his horn. The air gets tense.*) Where do you think you are going, Kaya?

KAYA (*not looking at him*). It's unfair, Bro Menzi. When you say your poems, we don't interfere. But you want to tell us how to play.

MENZI. Oh, I've paid you for a few sessions and now you think you are a big shot?! You think you are Sonny Rollins or . . . or Mankunku Ngozi! Let me tell you something for nothing boy—you are nothing! Nothing! I found you starving to death in that *shebeen kwa* Mona Lisa *e* Orlando East, and I made you a person—*ndakwenz' umntu. Awuyaz' ishow Bizz, izakunyisa.*[4] You think I don't know what I'm talking about? Boy, I've been in show business long before you were born. I hung around cats back in the day. (*Kaya is folding his music stand and collecting his score sheets. Menzi turning to the bass player*) I'm talking about fine cats, boy, *Abo*-Mackay Davashe, Mongezi Feza, Cyril Magubane, Ernest Motlhe, and the Heshoo Beshoo band. Those were fine cats. (*Kaya walks out.*)

You play a few scales and you think you have arrived? Music is big and vast, boy. This generation *ye toyi-toyi nicinga ukuba* you know.[5] Sit down and let me tell you that you don't know a thing. Art is not about ego and throwing your weight around. Art is about humility, *ubuntu*,[6] and service to the human race. Love for humanity. *Lentwana icinga ukuba i*clever.[7] He'll come crawling back in here, you mark my words. Come on, let's do this shit.

---

2 Finish and made up!

3 And you, what the hell are you talking about?

4 You don't know showbiz, it'll make you shit bricks.

5 This *toyi-toyi* generation, you think you know. ("*Toyi-toyi*" refers to a political dance expressing defiance and mimicking gestures of warfare. It was used in street demonstrations during the struggle against apartheid.)

The bass and the piano do a duet and Menzi continues with the poem. They fade as lights go out.

Scene 3

An irate Lady enters the living room, Bonga follows nonchalantly. She throws her bag and a bunch of house keys on the sofa. Bonga looks uneasy as he takes off his jacket and throws it on the sofa.

LADY. Did you really have to create a scene? (*Bonga does not answer but throws himself on the sofa.*) We were having such a great time until you spoiled it. Sometimes, I wonder why is it that you can't let people have fun without causing a war.

BONGA (*getting irked*). We were having a friendly argument, I mean . . . discussion.

LADY. Do you call that a discussion? You made the poor soul feel sorry for his beliefs, and all that in front of his wife and child.

BONGA (*breaking into a mocking laugh*). Oh, all of a sudden Bafana is a poor soul.

LADY. Laugh, *hleka, kumnandi kuwe angithi*?[8]

BONGA. Lady, what's wrong with you?

LADY. What's wrong with me? What's wrong with you! We went out to Bafana and Nomsa's house to have fun with them, like good neighbors, and you, the honorable Bonga Miya spoiled it all. Just say thanks that Bafana is a gentleman of excellent breeding—if *bekuyimi*,[9] I would have told you where to get off.

BONGA. You are just worked-up for nothing—we were just having a men's talk, men talking.

LADY. You call that "just having a men's talk?" Let me tell you what you did. You insulted Bafana. If I were you, I would pick up that phone right now and apologize.

BONGA. Over my dead body! Apologize for my views? Lady, come on!

---

6 . . . a collective sense of humanity, . . .

7 This boy thinks he's clever.

8 . . . , it's all nice to you, isn't it?

9 . . . —if it were me, . . .

LADY. You made Bafana feel small for being a Seventh Day Adventist. You called their church a leftover from a tired American spiritual banquet. How do you think that made him feel? Ha? *Nogal*[10] in front of his wife and child. That family takes their religion seriously. You hurt their feelings, and you know it too.

BONGA. All I was saying was that the world is not 6,000 years old, as he maintains. There is archeological evidence that the world is billions and billions of years old.

LADY. You were not listening to him. He was not refuting that. All he was saying was that when God created the world, he obviously created things with an impression of time. When Adam was created on the first day, he had an impression of a full-grown man and yet it was his first day on the planet. So were the rocks, which could have borne evidence of billions of years on their first day. (*There is silence.*) Obviously, his argument is light years ahead of your poetic logic.

BONGA. If you find Bafana's argument so wonderful, what are you making all this noise for?

LADY (*placating*). I am not making noise, honey. I saw how their faces looked, disappointed and hurt. You don't go into someone's house and start undermining their very existential beliefs. Bafana and Nomsa met at their annual camp meeting; they got married properly in a church by a pastor. (*In great anger, Bonga grabs his jacket*) Where are you going, Bonga?

BONGA. Come, let's go.

LADY. Where?

BONGA. I'm going to find a Seventh Day Adventist pastor and then marry you properly in a church.

LADY. Honey, you are missing the point. I am the one who said we should go and sign at the Home Affairs Offices remember?

BONGA. *Ja.* But now it seems you regret the fact that you were not married in a church like Bafana and Nomsa.

LADY. I do not regret a thing with you, honey. All I'm saying is that their church means a lot to them and you should respect that. Bonga, I knew when we got married that you were a struggling artist, and that we both did not have

---

10 And also . . .

enough money to throw a big party for our wedding celebration. I love my life with you. Every day is like a wedding party with you. (*Lady takes his jacket and kisses him, and he kisses her back.*) You know something? It would please me so much if you picked up that phone, dialed Bafana's number and told him you are sorry for what happened tonight. (*Takes Bonga's jacket and her bag to the bedroom, leaving Bonga staring contemplatively at the phone.*)

By and by he picks up the phone, dials the number and waits.

BONGA. Mr. Modiri . . .

BAFANA. Mr. Miya sir . . . are you safely home?

BONGA. We are safely home. (*Lady stands at the door, watches Bonga.*) Listen man . . .

BAFANA. Yes, Mr. Miya.

BONGA. We had a great time with my wife in your house.

BAFANA. No, say it right brother Bonga. I had a great time with my wife in your company. I was just telling my wife that you guys are like family. We should have more of these . . .

BONGA. Bafana, I'm sorry man about what I said tonight about your religious principles.

BAFANA. What are you talking about? We were having a friendly debate, brother.

BONGA. I thought so too at the time. But now, I know it wasn't a good call to go as far as I did.

BAFANA. You are a kind man, Brother Bonga.

BONGA. Give my love to little Lerato and Nomsa. Good night.

BAFANA. Good night.

Bonga turns and holds out the phone to Lady. She walks to him and kisses him as lights go out on them.

Scene 4

The band is playing "Esapha"[11] *as Menzi performs a poem.*

MENZI. Wish I could dance like a poet
Waltz on one leg across the paper's cape

---

11 "*Esapha*" is an ancient sacred place of AmaXhosa deities. AmaXhosa is the second largest ethnic group in South Africa.

Leaving immortal stains with each twist
And muted words that echo eternally

A poet I wish I was
Rich with metaphor, keen of insight
Slow to speak, wary of empty thoughts
Quick to inspire

Since I'm not one,
Me thinks to do what others do
Envy the poet, his skill and mystique
Clap along as he dances below crescent moons
Telling tales untold yet
Giving all, to all, always
All alone

Poets and prophets run far and long
Along pathways that stretch and twist
Among people who scorn and wrong
Yet their every step shrugs age
And their utterances inspire still

When alone they see things
That words struggle to tell
And this be their burden
To make words tell
To give meaning to life
In words

They pay for the sins of the world
Sing in the sixth voice
And dance in writhing rhythms
That melt hearts and dry rivers

Give me the spirit of an eagle
Give me the freshness of a dewdrop
So I can speak words that soar to the moon
Yet forever ready to drop at dawn
On a dry township peach tree
Perched discordantly before a grotesque four-roomed house.

Bonga enters, his poetry manuscript in hand. Menzi sees him and his face radiates with joy.

Ladies and gents, I have to welcome a young lion of the pen, a restless predator that prowls the night, pilfering words and setting the world on fire. As always, I know he has something for us tonight. Give it up for Bonga!

Bonga and Menzi hug. As Menzi goes to sit and Bonga mounts the bandstand, they look at each other with that esprit de corps *typical only among good friends. Bonga recites the poem.*

BONGA. Once I knew a poet
    Black, brisk, and crisp in his prime
    Made folks stop and stoop at his words
    Had them walk away in silence
    Heads drooping, eyes blinking
    His words clinging to their frocks
    A murderous testament of a blessing and a curse

    I met him again after many moons
    Limping in Hillbrow alleyways
    From rubbish bin to refuse bag
    Hunkering sadly like a wounded lion
    He looked at me with eyes of age
    I surprised weariness in them

    People greeted him, some making fun of his wanting state
    Never said a word but walked on dazed
    His lights had long been switched off God knows where

    And I wished I were a poet
    To give him a word or two
    For this was his tragedy
    This was his death

    Living in a world
    Raped of meaning
    Raped of words

    Bonga joins Menzi.

MENZI. You're getting better all the time. That was good, really.

BONGA. Thank you. What can I say? I learn from the master himself.

They both laugh. Menzi notices that Bonga is not quite himself.

MENZI. Boy, what's wrong?

BONGA. I'm fine, Bro Menzi.

MENZI. *Andiyokwekwe kwedini tyhin!* I can see you are not fine. *Yintoni? Kutheni?*[12]

There is an uncomfortable silence as Menzi awaits the answer.

BONGA. My poetry manuscript has just been rejected.

Menzi looks at him with great compassion. Grief-stricken, Bonga walks away from him.

MENZI. Now that sucks. But you've got to take it, boy, take it like a man. If you can't take the shame of being a writer, then you are not fit to receive its glory. The path to success is long and winding. And scattered with thorns. (*Silence*) What are you going to do now? (*Silence*) You can't stop now—you've gone too far.

BONGA. I think I'm going to do exactly that. White people think I'm too black in my writing, black people say I'm writing outdated protest poetry. What I don't understand is that when Jews write about the Holocaust, when they make films about it, nobody says they are writing about outdated issues.

MENZI. You can say anything, Bonga, be it old or new. Its not what you say, its in the how. You think what made me is something new? No! Nothing's new under the sun. We are saying the same old shit, in new ways though.

BONGA. I'm finished, Bro Menzi, I'm finished.

MENZI. Boy, you haven't even started yet. Give that manuscript. I'll talk to my publishers in Amsterdam.

As Menzi browses through the manuscript, Bonga looks at him with wonder.

BONGA. Bro Menzi?

MENZI. What?

BONGA. You will do that for me?

MENZI. Come, let's have a drink. What would you like?

The pianist starts an intro to "Thula"[13] *as they talk softly. Kaya enters, he looks ragged and unkempt and is carrying a Checkers*[14] *plastic bag. The band stops playing. Menzi looks at him questioningly.*

---

12 I am not a boy, young man! . . . What is it? What happened?
13 "Hush now."

KAYA. Bro Menzi . . . *kush' ukuthi*[15] . . .

The pianist starts the intro.

MENZI (*to the pianist*). Just stop that for a while, please. (*To Kaya*) *Kush' ukuthini?*[16]

KAYA. I'm sorry, Bro Menzi.

There is silence as Menzi takes a long hard look at Kaya.

MENZI. Where's your horn? (*Kaya does not answer.*) *He kwedini* I said *iphi* I horn *yakho? Akuva ngendlebe?*[17]

KAYA. *Ise* pawn shop *e* Hillbrow.[18]

MENZI. Look at you. Just take a look at you. What's wrong with you, boy? A whole Selma in a pawnshop? *E* Hillbrow of all places. They will sell it for a song because they don't even know what a Selma is. (*Silence as Menzi looks pitifully at Kaya.*) I have to get that horn out, Bonga. Have a drink on me— I'll see you later. Guys, let's call it a day.

The piano starts an intro to "Thula" and the bass joins in.

Scene 5

The band plays "Emzantsi"[19] *on a dark stage. Lights come up on Bonga and Lady's living room. We see Lady seated, reading a magazine. Bonga runs in sweating and almost out of breath.*

BONGA. Lady!

LADY. *Yini*, Bonga?[20]

BONGA. The radio! (*He looks for it frantically.*)

LADY. What?

BONGA. There is an important interview on the radio. Where is the damn radio?

Lady gets the portable radio, Bonga grabs it from her and turns the dial. They both sit down to listen. As the tune winds down to a pianissimo, Sbongile, the radio host for the "Rush Hour" program on Radio Thetha, is heard on the airwaves.

---

14 One of South Africa's leading supermarkets.

15 . . . I want to . . .

16 What is it?

17 Boy, I said where's your horn?

18 In the pawnshop at Hillbrow.

SBONGILE (*v/o*). Thisssss is the Rrrrrradio Thththethetha, the "Conscience of the Nation"—"Rushhhh Hour" with your host—Sbongile behind the mike. Welcome, welcome and welcome. With me in the studio today is the one and only, the maestro, the word-spinner—affectionately known as Bro Menzi. Welcome to Radio Thetha, Bro Menzi.

A spotlight slowly comes up on Menzi who is seated on a stool with headphones on.

MENZI. Thank you.

SBONGILE (*v/o*). This is your first radio interview?

MENZI. Yes.

SBONGILE (*v/o*). In the 30 years you've been a writer, you have written three novels, six stage plays and two collections of poetry. And in all this time you have never given a radio interview—why?

MENZI. For a number of reasons, chief among being that I am very shy and that I had not forgiven myself for what happened to my mother 20 years ago. When I left home in the Eastern Cape, my mother was sick in bed. I left her with my brother, *u* Themba, and two younger sisters, *u* Mhiza *no* Vuyokazi.[21] In my bag were a few shirts, a black comb, and an unfinished manuscript of my first novel—*When I'm Gone, Tell My Story In B Flat Blues*.

SBONGILE (*v/o*). So, that was the last time you saw her, your mother?

MENZI. Yes. And I knew that the life I had chosen had gotten the better of her. It took me years to forgive myself. I had a love–hate relationship with my writings. I lived with the truth that these books had cost me my mother, and, after all the toil and blues, I still wonder if it was worth all the pain and loss.

SBONGILE (*v/o*). So, have you seen your brother and two sisters?

MENZI. They are the only family I have, and I make sure that I see them all the time.

SBONGILE (*v/o*). Your last book, a collection of your poems, is dedicated to all the single people in the world.

MENZI. Yes.

---

19 "In the South of Africa."
20 Yes, Bonga?
21 . . . Mhiza and Vuyokazi.

BONGO. Why?

MENZI. I think marriage sucks. I was never cut out for it. And besides, as an institution, it is very flawed and nonsensical.

SBONGILE (v/o). What do you mean?

MENZI. Look, today when you wake up in the morning, you wake up in a twenty-first-century bed, you take a bath in a twenty-first-century bathroom, you walk out of a twenty-first-century house into a twenty-first-century car. The roads, the bridges are twenty-first-century designs. You walk into a twenty-first-century building with the latest technology to resume a day's work. Your children are exposed to twenty-first-century thoughts and TV programs. Everything, I mean everything, is twenty-first-century friendly, except for one thing—the marriage institution. It is the only cave practice that man has dragged from the dark yesterdays into the blinding light of today. It is an old and tired shoe that no one can fit into. You are exposed to a twenty-first-century lifestyle, all new, and in the middle of all that you want to fit in marriage. It cannot work. That is why it is falling apart. That is the logical conclusion.

SBONGILE (v/o). But there are people who are happily married.

MENZI. Yes, of course there are. Two-thirds of the world is made up of people who are still scared of the monster in the dark, *boyik' irhorho*.[22] If you are still scared of *irhorho*, then marriage is good for you—obviously, you will be happily married.

SBONGILE (v/o). There has been a concern in newspapers and other media about your performances in bars and *shebeen*s. The general feeling is that you confine yourself to a particular audience that is not very representative of the people.

MENZI. That issue is very simple. When I first came here, the only people who embraced me were the very people you find in jazz bars and *shebeen*s.

SBONGILE (v/o). As far as you can see today, Bro Menzi, where is the literary current headed?

MENZI. There is definitely a move towards a new direction although it is not perceived to be progressive by new South African standards. There's this young man, I'm sure you've heard of him, *u* Bonga Miya. He performs

---

22 Monster—they are scared of the monster.

mainly in jazz clubs. I think he is a significant voice that is struggling to get published. His themes revolve around the proud history of black people, especially in South Africa. That according to me is a significant step as it places black people in their rightful place of pride and dignity. I have a poem by him here with me. Can I read just a stanza or two?

SBONGILE (*v/o*). Yes, sure, Bro Menzi, go ahead, this is your show.

MENZI. Blues sprouting from my black scalp
Cascading down my locks onto my back
Winding through the maze of my black skin
For I am black and the blues knows it

Black blues that failed to break Luthuli
And stifled not Biko's beautiful black spirit
Blues that turned black in a river of song and dance
Black, I am black, and the blues knows it right

Lights slowly go out on Menzi and we hear a brief saxophone solo. Bonga switches the radio off.

BONGA. He's such a great man.

LADY. *Ja*, and just as sick.

BONGA. Lady!

LADY. A sick man like that and you call him a great man—please, come on, you can do better than that. (*Silence.*) Listen to his views about marriage. We are a married couple, Bonga. He is desecrating everything we stand for. The Bible says marriage is holy and he says it sucks—please!

The phone rings and Lady answers.

NOSMA (*v/o, very excited*). Hi, sister Lady!

LADY. Hi, Nomsa *kunjani?*[23]

NOSMA (*v/o*). I'm sorry if you are busy with something but . . .

LADY. No, feel free, I'm not busy.

NOSMA (*v/o*). *Phela u*[24] Lerato has just surprised us. She just sang a song from a CD *ye Joyous Celebration*. (*To Lerato*) *Woza uzoculela u sisi* Lady, baby, *woza.*[25]

---

23 . . . how's it?
24 By the way . . .
25 Come sing for sis' Lady, baby, come.

LERATO (*v/o*). *Uzongipha i* ice-cream *e fridgini kena* Mama?[26]

NOSMA. *Yebo ngizokupha woza.*[27]

LERATO (*v/o*). I want to be ready,
  I want to be ready
  I want to be ready
  To walk in Jerusalem
  Just like John (x2)

  (*When Lerato repeats the first stanza, Lady gestures for Bonga to join her and he does. They both break into soft smiles as they listen to Lerato's rendition.*)

  Three gates in the east
  Three gates in the west
  Three gates in the south
  Three gates in the north
  Twelve gates to the city
  Twelve gates to the city
  To walk in Jerusalem
  Just like John

NOMSA (*v/o*). We didn't know that she knew the words so well . . .

LADY. What a voice, Nomsa.

NOMSA (*v/o*). *Siyabonga* sis' Nomsa.[28]

BONGA (*to Nomsa*). Now I know I'm not the only artist on the block.

We hear Nomsa laughing and the line dying.

LADY. Oh, she is so sweet. I can't wait for my own.

BONGA. You are not starting that now, are you?

LADY. Honey, two years is too long to wait. Why can't we have a child sooner than that?

Bonga takes out his books and starts jotting things down. Lady gives him a disgruntled look as she exits. Lights slowly go out on him. The band plays "Bro Pat."

---

26 Will you give me some ice-cream, Mama?
27 Yes I will, come now.
28 Thank you, Sister Nomsa.

Scene 6

Bar. Bonga is performing a poem.

BONGA. My father wore brown suede shoes
 That made my mother look long and hard
 Whenever he walked out the door

 My father wore brown suede shoes
 That made children freeze at play
 And mothers suspend their gossip
 Whenever he swaggered by

 Lexington ash soiled the suede shoes
 And smoke swirled teasing curls
 to form a flight of stairs for some wanton lover
 Beguiled by the brown suede shoes

 My father wore brown suede shoes
 Crossed legs like Armstrong's bended horn
 While he tapped blithely
 to Satchmo's Good Book blues

 My father has since passed on
 And my mother at length
 gave me the brown suede shoes

 I now wear the brown suede shoes
 Yet cannot tell a trumpet from a sax
 Nor can I swagger or jitterbug
 But heads turn whenever I cut a corner
 I guess it's the brown suede shoes

MENZI. *Qula Kwedini!*[29] Boy, you look good, what's happening?

They both laugh heartily.

BONGA. That was a beautiful poem, Bro Menzi. It deserves a round, on me.

Menzi's mood softens somewhat and he gets teary.

MENZI. You look great. What would you like to drink?

BONGA. Question is, what would you like to drink?

---

29 Do it, young man!

MENZI. Boy, what's going on here? Are you shining on me? *Uyaqhoma?*[30] (*Bonga takes out a brown envelope and gives it to Menzi. Menzi is surprised and hesitantly opens it. He is taken aback*) What's this for?

BONGA. For you?

MENZI. Why?

BONGA. You put in a good word for me, remember? And now, because of a recommendation from the maestro himself, they are going to publish my poetry.

MENZI. What are you saying to me?

BONGA. *Ja.*

Menzi takes a long hard look at Bonga before they both burst out laughing and hug. They get their drinks and sit down.

MENZI. Now, you got to listen carefully. You are a big boy now, that's all right. You got to guard against too much self-pity in your writing, it's not good. Keep your work serious but light. Publishers will tell the same thing. People out there don't want to read all that sordid and grim literature. Let your work be a beam of light, keep away from depressing themes. Hear me?

BONGA. Sure.

MENZI. Then you'll be made. (*Menzi lifts his glass*) To the new kid on the block! *They toast.*

Scene 7

The band is playing "Love Birds." Bonga enters carrying a colorful and glossy paper bag.

BONGA. Lady, Lady, Lady, baby!

Bonga throws the bags onto the couch. Lady enters, yawns and her face breaks into a soft smile.

LADY. Where have you been? I've been waiting for you.

BONGA. I'm here, babes, and you know what? I'm all yours, from the north of my head to the south of my shoes. (*He kisses her.*) You look tired and hungry. Have you eaten?

---

30 Are you bragging?

LADY. I've been waiting for you. I'm sure that food is cold. What took you so long?

BONGA. You on my mind.

LADY. *Ag suka*[31] man, Bonga I'm serious. And what's all this now? (*They both walk toward the couch. Lady peeps through the paper bag and her face lights up immediately.*) Bonga! Who are these for?

BONGA. Some fine lady I'm crazy about.

LADY. Bonga man *awuyekel'ukudlala.*[32]

BONGA. Wait, wait, wait let me tell you about her. She is a lady, right? Walks like the world owes her a couple o' million rand. Talks so fine, like an African princess. (*Lady starts smiling*) Her smile is like a crack on a full moon broken by the gods at dawn for breakfast. See her looking at me now and you'll know why I'm so crazy about her.

Lady is overcome by emotion. She hugs him and takes the items from the bags one at a time.

LADY. Look at this! How did you know that I needed this? Oh, Bonga!

BONGA. What?

LADY. This is . . . Baby, you are going to make me cry. (*She takes a good long look at him, draws closer and hugs him.*) You know something?

BONGA. What?

The piano plays an intro to "I Feel So Wonderful" and Lady sings.

LADY. I feel so wonderful
I feel so good
He thinks I'm beautiful
Oh what a dude

Heaven comes right down
When he's around
Love has smiled on me

These things go to my head
They make me smile alone

---

31 Leave me alone . . .
32 Bonga, stop playing games, man.

My yesterdays were sad
Today I'm all smiles

Heaven comes right down
When he's around
Love has smiled on me

(*Refrain*) I never knew the wonders of love
Till that day he said hello
How could I know how could I tell
That love would smile on me
Life is a wonderland
My fairy tales are real
I'm in a carousel
I'm spinning round and round
He brings me happiness
He makes me laugh
Love has smiled on me

BONGA. That was . . . thanks.

LADY. I love this man.

BONGA. I love you too.

LADY. I mean it, Bonga. I don't know what I did to have such a caring man in my life. You make me feel as if I'm the only living creature on the planet.

BONGA. You are the only lovely being on my planet.

LADY. I feel so loved. Bring that black face here. (*She kisses him and goes back to the lingerie he bought her. She takes one more look at them before wrapping them up and placing them into the bag.*) I like it when you spoil me like this.

BONGA. You are always complaining because I'm never home. That bugs me.

LADY. I thought you didn't care.

BONGA. Of course I care—what do you mean?

LADY. I know, I know, I know you care. (*She kisses him.*) Now, the million dollar question: Where did you get the money?

BONGA. An advance from the publishers, Amsterdam. The poetry manuscript, remember?

LADY. The publishers here did not even want to read it?

BONGA. I know. I spoke to Menzi and he put in a good word for me with his publishers in Amsterdam. They listened to him because he is . . . you know, the best in the country.

LADY. And?

BONGA. They spend some time reading it and it turns out they like the work.

LADY. Just like that?

BONGA. Just like that.

LADY. Now, were you not supposed to spend the money on the book? You know . . .

BONGA. I know.

LADY. And so?

BONGA. Why am I working, Lady? Why am I spending all those long hours on writing? (*Pause*) So we can have a better life. A good life. And a good life to me is when you are happy, when you have the things you desire.

LADY. Stop it.

BONGA. Why?

LADY. I like it.

They both laugh and kiss. Bonga grabs his jacket. He gives her a peck as he exits. The band plays "Inyibiba."[33]

Scene 8

The stage is dark. The sound of things falling and smashing and screaming voices cuts across the darkness. A man's voice is ordering everyone around, cursing in the process. A woman's voice is heard crying during a rape ordeal. A man's voice is pleading for the woman to no avail—the rapist is brutal, even in the dark. A young girl weeps sorrowfully.

RAPIST (*o/s*). Hey 'tsek wena nja![34]

WOMAN (*o/s*). Bafana! *Iyoo*[35] . . .

---

33 "*Lily*".
34 Hey, shut up dog!
35 Help . . .

MAN (o/s). *Ma* Gents *ngiyacela* man please, *yi vrou phela lena. Oku ngcono cishani mina ke.*[36]

RAPIST (o/s). Hey *thula wena nja!*[37]

LITTLE GIRL (o/s). Mama! Mama!

RAPIST (o/s). Hey *wena sfebe! Awusheshe isikhathi sishwabenephela.*[38]

MAN (o/s). *Awu magents phela ngiyacela*[39] . . .

Scene 9

Lady and Bonga are standing in the kitchen, looking crestfallen. Two bowls of cereal and a pint of milk are waiting on the table. There is heavy silence in the air. When Bonga breaks the silence, Lady speaks too and they simultaneously stop talking.

BONGA. When did this happen?

LADY. They say around two o'clock in the morning.

Silence.

BONGA. I think I heard a few gunshots last night while we were at the bar.

LADY. To think that I was right here and I never even heard a sound. Where were you? (*She starts sobbing.*)

Bonga comforts her, helps her to a seat. He takes a bowl of cereal and gives it to her.

BONGA. You have to eat, Lady.

LADY. But why did they kill them? Okay, they took everything in the house, they raped Nomsa in front of her child and husband, and, as if that was not enough, they kill them. (*Silence. Lady starts sobbing, Bonga comforts her.*) I'm scared, Bonga.

BONGA. It's all right.

LADY. No, it's not all right. How could you say that?

BONGA. I don't mean . . .

---

36 Gents, I'm asking you, please, this is my wife. Rather kill me then.
37 Shut up, you dog!
38 Bitch! Quick, time's gone!
39 Please, gents.

LADY. What do you mean? They were our neighbors. Do you realize that it could have been us last night? It could have been me since you were not even here when this happened. (*Silence*) This manuscript is turning out to be a curse. If you are not spending time writing, you are getting the coaching from that maestro—getting all the bad influence. I hate him.

BONGA. It's not a nice thing to say. Besides, you don't even know him.

LADY. He's changed you. Can't you see?

BONGA. That's an insult.

LADY. You've been acting strange since you've been with him—you've changed. Your neighbors just got killed last night and all you can think of is going to that poet. (*Silence*) You are never home, Bonga. You're just never home.

BONGA. Oh . . .

LADY. What's the point of us lying to ourselves thinking that we stay together when in fact we are just strangers who happen to share the same apartment?! To tell you the truth, I don't see any difference between us and commuters on a train to Cofimvaba.

BONGA. So, what are you going to do?

LADY. What do you mean what am I going to do? You are the one who's never home, you are the one with the problem—don't shift it over to me.

BONGA. You are getting it all wrong. You are the one who's got a problem with my job. I'm a poet, remember? I work in pubs and rowdy jazz clubs. It's tough sometimes but that's the life I chose for myself. I like it with all that it brings. I'm not complaining. I take it. It's what I decided to do with my life.

LADY. You said things were going to be better and we would spend more time together.

BONGA. Yes I said that but . . .

LADY. You promised, Bonga! You promised!

BONGA. I don't control these things. People give me awkward time slots and I don't have a choice but to fit into their schedules or stay without a job. I know I want to make things better for us, that's why I lied and said things would be better. But the truth is, nothing's going to get better. You have to get used to the fact that you are staying with an artist who keeps awkward working hours and try and find it in your heart to make peace with that.

LADY. Why do I always have to try and try? You never do anything to make things better. I'm the one who's got to understand, try, fit into your life, do this, do that.

BONGA. I'm not the one who's complaining. You are the one . . .

LADY. Bonga, do you realize that I nearly got raped and killed last night and you were not home?

BONGA. *Ja.*

LADY. So what are you *gaaning aan* about?[40] All you think of is your writing and that maestro poet of yours. *Ag suka* man. (*Exits.*)

The band plays "Blue Over Brown."

Scene 10

Jazz bar. The band is playing "Mka."[41] Menzi is reciting a poem.

MENZI. Jazz frees my soul
From myself it liberates me
See me fall like a meteor beyond the sky
To hide beneath the cloud of a love supreme

Lakutshon'ilanga[42] put some jazz in my coffee
From a blue tumbler let me sip a moon river
A room full of blues, better still, cry me a river

When your lover has gone
You take giant steps
Drown in Scotch bottles
And bend over booze-stained tables
Sniffing deadly white powders
With godforsaken women

Yakhal'inkomo makwedini[43]
Well, the masquerade is over
I hope you remember those rainy nights

---

40 What are you going on about?
41 "Go away."
42 When the sun sets . . .
43 The cow is bellowing, young boys.

In Soweto, Gugulethu, Mlazi, Mamelodi
Almost like being in love
Hands reaching out between knocked knees
Cruising up and then choking
Making hard black love
Behind corrugated-iron shacks

Sing me softly of the blues
And speak low when you speak love
'Cause Soweto dawn is here, babe
Easy living, let's get lost
Just don't take my money
Come taste my honey

Give me some jazz 'round midnight
When you roll over to give me your jewels
Wrapped up in red satin, cushioned in black velvet
Quick, girl, the night has a thousand eyes
And the sun don't lie

Run me a blues line at dawn
Before you call the angel of the morning
Before you say—good morning, heartache,
Don't smoke in bed
'Cause I've got it bad and that ain't good

Some black girl is all alone tonight, thinking—
"I'm gonna sit right down and write me a letter
It don't mean a thing if it ain't got that swing"
Some day my prince will come
I'll holler take five while I cruise my blues on the A Train
What is this thing called love?

Time now for tough talk
The thrill is gone
There is no greater love
There will never be another you
The midnight train's gone!

Bonga enters; Menzi is excited to see him, but realizes Bonga is not his usual self.

What's wrong predator? Lion that prowls the deep nights searching for fat words?

BONGA. Why do we write books and poems?

MENZI. What are you talking about?

BONGA. I mean, why do you write?

MENZI. I'm a writer, man, what else do you want me to be? A train-driver?

BONGA. What do you hope to achieve with your writing? Except critical acclaim and popularity?

MENZI. What the hell are you on about tonight?

BONGA. My neighbor was murdered last night. His little girl was killed too. Before they killed him, it is alleged that he had to watch his woman get raped, and then killed.

Silence.

MENZI. I heard about it, man. All I can say is that I'm sorry. There's nothing we can do about it, man, except getting all worked up. Your job and mine is to write, not get worked up by situations beyond our control. As a writer, you need your wits about you. You cannot afford to get easily worked up. Keep a level head, stay calm.

Bonga calms down.

BONGA. My woman is worried sick, she's scared, man. Now she thinks that if I'm home all the time, these things won't happen to us. And that's bullshit. If all women in this country are living in fear, how the hell can she hope to live in peace simply because I'm there?

An awkward silence.

MENZI. Come, let me get you something to drink?

BONGA. I don't need a drink, Bro Menzi.

MENZI. My *laaitie*, you are not a politician. Let them fix the filth they created in the first place. What do you want to do? Fix the world? When I was younger, I saw so many wrong things in the world and I set out to fix them. But then I realized that the world was too big and too wrong and powerful and I was just all alone, defeated long before I even started. (*Silence*) When is the funeral?

BONGA. On Sunday. (*Silence*) They were Seventh Day Adventists, went to church on Saturday. I'll see you, Bro Menzi. I have to go.

Scene 11

The bass plays a solo on "Mka." On stage are three coffins created by light and a blue spotlight. Bonga walks to the spotlight.

BONGA. I am today supposed to speak over the lifeless body of this young family—Bafana Modiri, Nomsa, his wife, and their beautiful little girl, Lerato. It seems like yesterday when I argued with Bafana over ideas and visions we had in this life but could never come to any agreement; I can almost see Nomsa across the room, looking at her husband, her face brimming with affection for him; Lerato, their sprightly daughter, bringing down heaven into that home. But all that was yesterday—today they lie here before us, tearing our hearts so and bringing tears to our eyes. I am supposed to say something. And I don't know what to say. Am I supposed to say rest in peace my bro, *sobonana kwelizayo?*[44] But we all know that I cannot say such a thing. He will never rest in peace. He died a horrible death, screaming like a goat, begging for the life of his loved ones in the hands of a merciless mob. They emptied their bullets into his chest while his wife and child helplessly looked on. As if that was not enough, they went on and raped Nomsa while her little girl stood there crying. The little girl looked on as they took turns on her mother. She looked on as her mother gasped for breath because she could not cry any more. She saw too, when the men dragged her mother around, blood running between her legs—her mother's blood writing things on the carpet. I imagine the little girl shocked at the horrible face of the world, the world we have created. She beheld this spectacle, her eyes not blinking. And when her mother gave her last breath, the little girl felt something strange move inside her chest—little did she know that she was feeling, for the first time, prematurely, what it is like to be a woman today in our new democratic South Africa. Angry, bitter, and helpless at the hands of the male species. Then they shot her in the head and left with her father's car. Now the blood of this young family is testament to the whirlwind that this nation will reap for its fascination with blood and the death of the innocent. We will live to reap the bitter fruit in our children. For these children see too much blood. Blood and killing! They read bloody news from blood-soaked newspapers, blood dripping from blazing television sets. Blood, blood, blood! God gave us a beautiful flower in this little girl lying here today, but we

---

44 We'll meet again in the next life.

nipped it in the bud. She was a promise of things to come. We were still expecting to see the flower bloom at the break of dawn. But they got her at midnight and cut her. And, at dawn, the world will never know of the splendor trapped in this little girl. I know you want fashionable speakers with fashionable speeches for a fashionable people with a fashionable sickness. I know, for I too used to be fashionable and you loved me so. Oh, how you loved me. You bought me presents, took me to your dining tables and fed me all sorts of meats and dumplings. You loved me and lifted me up high and sang my praises. Yes, you loved me for saying the things you wanted to hear. Things that tickled your ears and promised peace, stability, and prosperity. Things that troubled not the waters. Nice things. I am tired of it all. I am tired of whispering sweet nothings into your ears. (*By now the band is cooking up a storm in the background. Bonga turns and addresses the band.*) Stop it! This is no time for sweet melodies!

The band stops playing.

I am tired of your meats and dumplings. In fact, I have since become a vegetarian. Tired of your worthless feasts bought at a heavy price. *Maaka! Loleme!*[45] Lies! What kind of people are you? They were only starting out. They were young and promised so much. What sort of a nation is this that is not moved by death? What future is there for your children? Your children are wild and shifty. Their hearts have been charred in angry flames. They kill like this (*snapping fingers*) and they die just like that. But I tell you—you have nothing as a people if you don't have a heart. (*Pause.*)

One day, Jesus saw women crying over the death of Lazarus. And Jesus wept. The gods weep every time we kill. They weep, for they know the grief caused by death. They weep, for they understand how helpless humanity is in the face of death. And this nation kills at random every day. Now lift up your heads and behold the works of your own hands. Here they are, Bafana, Nomsa, and Lerato, lifeless before this nation. They faced your brutality head on. I hope you take it too when your turn comes.

The bass plays a solo.

---

45 Lies! Gossip!

Scene 12

In the jazz bar Menzi is reciting a poem while Bonga and Lady are making love in their apartment on the couch.

MENZI. The sun stole the glow in your eyes
   The rose got its color from your heart
   Honey kissed you and has never tasted the same since
   The seas heard of you in their sleep
   And have been galloping ever since
   And when the night first saw you,
   She giggled and twinkled and yawned
   And wrapped you in her nocturnal blanket
   Hiding you from the blinding glow of dawn
   So you wet my forlorn eyes
   Like crystal dewdrops on parched orchards
   At noon azure sheets unfurl to reveal you
   And the sun stoops down, taking sips of you
   To cool her burning face
   And when you caught my eye, girl I died a little
   Blinding light of a luminous star
   Kissed only by the sun

LADY. I'm sorry about the other day. (*Silence*) Bonga?

BONGA. What?

LADY. Say something.

BONGA. What do you want me to say?

LADY. I said, I'm sorry about what I said to you.

BONGA. I'm sorry too.

LADY. That was a great speech you gave at the funeral. I couldn't help but feel proud of you.

BONGA. It was not meant for that.

LADY. Why are you so grumpy? What's wrong with saying thank you?

BONGA. I gave that speech because I was trying to reach people's hearts, to change something.

LADY. But dear, you can only do so much, the rest is up to the people.

BONGA. Suddenly, everyone thinks I'm a great writer because of that speech. I wasn't trying to be smart. All I was trying to do was make people rethink their behavior, their ways of doing things. All they see is the beauty of the words, not what they say.

LADY. Bonga, you can't bring them back. They are dead.

BONGA. Oh, now you're no longer saying it could have been you, us?

LADY. Yes, but . . .

BONGA. It's time someone told black people where to get off. (*Agitated. He exits.*)

Lady tries unsuccessfully to plead with him.

LADY. Bonga, please. Bonga! Bonga!

The band plays "Ikude."[46]

Scene 13

Bonga is a guest on Radio Thetha. He is seated on a barstool under a spotlight. He is the only person we see in this scene, all the other voices are off-stage, including Sbongile the "Rush Hour" host.

SBONGILE. You are tuned to Rrrrrradio Thththththetha, the "Conscience of the Nation." "Rrrrush Hour" with your host Sbo. With me in the studio is the new literary star on the block—the one and only Bonga Miya. There will be time for callers and the number is 089 8631719. Welcome Bonga to Radio Thetha, would you like to say "hi" to the listeners?

BONGA. Thank you, Sbongile. Hello, everybody.

SBONGILE. Let's start with your latest controversial claim that has the nation abuzz. You claim that black people essentially hate each other, right?

BONGA. That's right.

SBONGILE. What do you mean exactly?

BONGA. You see, Bongi, I never used to think about this thing in its true perspective until the tragic death of Bafana Modiri and his family. As you might have heard, they raped his wife in front of him and his little girl and then shot them. Now, this probably won't make sense if you've never known the man. He was my neighbor, a good neighbor at that. If you had known the

---

46 "*It's Far*".

man, his beaming face whenever he greeted you, his generosity and, oh yes, his beautiful love for his little girl and wife, you'd understand that he did not deserve the tragic end he had to meet. What kind of man would want to kill a man like that unless there's something horribly wrong with him?

SBONGILE. There are a number of callers on the line. Yes, Busi, are you there? Busi?

BUSI. Hello, Sbo, hello, Bonga.

SBONGILE. *Yebo*,[47] Busi.

BONGI. Hello.

BUSI. I just want to ask Bonga one question.

SBONGILE. Go ahead, my dear.

BUSI. Menzi is the best poet in the country at the moment. You are almost taking the limelight from him with your radical statements and especially your speech at the funeral. What do you think of his works? And how different is your work from his?

BONGA. Menzi is a good poet, he taught me many things but that's just about where it ends. We used to write in the same vein but I am now branching off in a different direction. I think it's okay to do ones poetry at jazz clubs and all that but to a limit. That is Menzi's problem. He has confined himself to the elite and the middle class and I don't find him shedding any new light in the development of the larger society. His writing serves the elite and has essentially nothing for the broader society. To be short, he has become too comfortable and I don't find him stretching the limits or breaking new ground.

SBONGILE. Thank you, Busi. Next caller on the line, Jack, are you there?

JABU. Sbo, *kunjani*?

SBONGILE. *Ngi* grand *mfo wethu*.[48] Do you have a comment or a question?

JABU. I've been listening to Bonga and as a Christian I would like to ask him a few questions.

SBONGILE. He's right here.

---

47 Yes . . .

48 I am grand, my brother.

JABU. *Kunjani* Bonga *mfowethu?*[49]

BONGA. *Ngi right gazi kunjani?*[50]

JABU. Sharp. Bonga, I don't understand half the things you are saying, especially about black people. From Biblical evidence we know that when Jesus was led to Golgotha, a black man helped him carry his cross. Moses's wife was black. There's a lot of evidence about the significant role of black people in the Bible and general history.

BONGA. As you say, it's all history. What I'm all about is—how is that history helping us to deal with the present as a black people? How is it taking us forward?

Silence.

You see, I don't blame you for not being able to answer that. Because it is all history and has very little to do with what we are today. What we have turned out to be cannot be traced back to the beautiful history you are talking about because that history is all nice and romantic, perhaps not as romantic as you would like to believe.

JABU. Bonga, our royalty as a black nation can be traced back to the history you call "all romantic." We cannot run away from who we used to be, we come from a great stock of innovators, scientists and thinkers. Well, I do agree that that is neither here nor there since it cannot be found today. But, how it was destroyed can only be traced back to history. Black people, especially in South Africa, have been brutalized by history. What black people are doing to each other is what they got fed. Their lives were rendered meaningless. Bonga, my Bro, if someone treats you as a meaningless entity for 300 years, you are bound to believe it. I am not condoning what we do to each other but life has become meaningless because our lives were meaningless.

BONGA. Hey, I think you have summarized today's topic. Let's pack our bags and go home. There is nothing we can do—the situation is hopeless. We are a sorry lot that has been brutalized by history. We bear scars of brutality. We can do no better in this life except brutality. I go on record tonight as saying I give black people a mandate never to rise above their history, to always remember their victim status. Of course, that is bullshit. It is a fact that we were once

---

49 How's it Bonga, my brother?
50 I'm all right, blood, how's it?

a people under siege. The question is: What are we going to do about it?

SBONGILE. Next caller on the line, yes, Mike?

MIKE. *Tankie ngoanake*,[51] Sbongile. Bonga, *ou seun*,[52] where do you go to church? *Kagonne ou seun oa bona Modimo otlile pele*.[53]

Ee,[54] I hear all what you young people are saying. *Wa bona*, I am not very *educatete nna*.[55] But as far as I can see, *le batla* peace *akere*?[56] What is strange is *le batla*[57] peace without inviting the prince of peace, Jesus Christ. If you want vitamin C, you have to eat an orange. *Beibele, ou seun*,[58] is the answer to perfect peace and security.

SBONGILE. Next caller on the line, hello, Mantwa.

MANTWA. Hello, Sbo, hello, Bonga. My name is Mantwa Diratsagae. I am the leader of Youth for Christ in the Southern Africa Region for the Salvation of the Black Population of Nazareth and Judea in the African Diaspora for the Restoration of the New Jerusalema, *mo* Klerksdorp.[59] We call ourselves YCSAR—

SBONGILE. What is your question, *Ous* Mantwa?[60]

MANTWA. *Kene kere hela*[61] I should give our name in short in case there are other people who are interested in our movement. We are YCSARSBNJADRNJ. My question is, Brother Bonga, do you ever write about hope, about God, and the meaning of life?

BONGA. My poetry is about God and the meaning of a God-less existence.

MANTWA. But are there no lighter shades in your understanding of life and God?

BONGA. Life has no shades. You create them. Life won't give you meaning. You have to create it or die. When God created the world, it was a beautiful par-

---

51 Thank you, Sbongile my child.
52 Bonga, old boy, . . .
53 Because old boy, you see, God came first.
54 Yes, . . .
55 You see, I am not very educated.
56 But as far as I can see you want peace, isn't it?
57 . . . you want . . .
58 The Bible, old boy, . . .
59 . . . in Klerksdorp.
60 . . . Sister Mantwa?
61 I was just saying . . .

adise with everything for everyone, but man destroyed all that. Now, everyone has to remake the world and invest it with their own meaning.

MANTWA. But if that is your view of the world, why don't you keep it to yourself? In the YCSARSBNJADRNJ we are trying to build the morale of black people and you are destroying it. People have their own opinions about the world and existence—they don't need you to tell them how to look at life.

BONGA. This world was created in broad daylight, in full view of the angels, and it was no secret when man decided to destroy it, and when we remake it, we do so unashamedly in full view of everyone. There is power in nakedness. "And He created them, man and woman, and they were naked and they were not ashamed." That's what I'm saying with my poetry—that black people have to start from the premise that they hate each other and then build from there. Look at the way black South Africans treat other blacks from the north of our borders. It's self-hatred.

MANTWA. So what about people like me who don't agree with your worldview?

BONGA. Hey, Mantwa, give me a break. I judge no one. The meaning of our lives is a judgment unto itself. When we give up the power to direct our lives to create our own meaning, we give up our only self-defining tool, OUR FREEDOM.

MANTWA. But why are you mixing the issue of rape with such grave matters?

BONGA. Isn't rape a serious issue?

MANTWA. Yes but . . .

BONGA. But what? The issue of rape is deeper than what happened to Bafana and his family. There's something that I can't put my finger on at the moment, but somebody will, I hope. It's something that happens when black people look at each other, I don't know what it is but I know it is not love, it's not even jealousy. It's something deeper, darker, and deadlier than the fear of the white man. Black people hate each other.

How do you explain the things we do to each other? We rape each other all the time. And when it happens physically, it's only a manifestation of a national psyche that's ruthless and poisonous.

MANTWA. But how do you get to such a sick conclusion about black people?

BONGA. How do you explain the turn of events in my popularity? I used to write about the greatness of a black people, their pride as a people, their ancient civilizations and all that. And I struggled to sell my books.

MANTWA. So you think they like you now because you've stopped saying they come from a great people, that they are the sons and daughters of kings and queens?

BONGA. Black people hated me for romanticizing their past, because it had nothing to do with who they are today. Deep down, they knew the truth and so did I. Maybe that's what they used to be. What they used to be and what they are now are two totally different things. And they like me now because what I say about them—although they won't admit it—they recognize as truth. Black people everywhere, and especially in South Africa, hate each other and why they've fooled the world about it is because they hide it behind their professed hatred for the white man. Black people won't let you forget how they hate the white man for what he did to them. But give them a gun and the truth comes out. Because the first person they'll point that same gun at is not the person they claim to hate, the white man. No!

SBONGILE. That was Mantwa, thank you Sister. Yes, Jack, you are on air, Rrrradio Thththtetha, the "Conscience of the Nation."

JACK. White people are also guilty of the very sin. They are killing each other as we speak. Look at Europe, the U.K., and America. Always scheming to get the better of each other.

BONGA. All the excuses in the world put together cannot condone what happened to Bafana and his family. If black people face up to the fact that they do hate each other, they will find the way to love each other, and half the crimes committed in this country will cease. Why do you want me to solve the atrocities in Kosovow? I'm starting at home first, right here where I live, then maybe I can move further afield.

JACK. Do you really believe what you just told me?

BONGA. Why did you want to talk to me in the first place? (*Silence*) I'll tell you why. Because my blatant truth strikes a chord with yours. Now you want to put me on your newspapers, you want to hear my voice on your radios. Why? Do you think it's a mistake? Chance or fate. And there is a myth that this hatred is found only among the poor and the downtrodden. Well, of course, the poor hate the black middle class because they envy their wealth. On the other hand, the black middle class hate the poor because the poor remind them of who they really are and what they could become if they slipped down too low; hence the vicious greed of the middle class. The hatred is everywhere among blacks—from parliament down to every church that's got black faces.

JACK. That includes you then.

BONGA. Yes.

Silence.

JACK. Do you hate black people, Bonga?

BONGA. I hate them for hating each other.

Sbongile cuts the dialogue.

SBONGILE. Thank you, Jack, time is up, brother. Last caller on the line. Yes Monde? Monde?

MONDE. Sbongile, that man is sick! What is his name again?

SBONGILE. Monde, you don't have to shout, we can hear you—

MONDE. How can a national radio allow such a mad person to address the nation? He should be in Sterkfontein—

SBONGILE. Monde, Monde listen—

MONDE. You are a danger to the black nation, you should be kill—

SBONGILE. Our time is over. Thank you, Bonga, for joining us.

BONGA. Thank you.

SBONGILE. I'm sorry about that.

Bonga laughs.

BONGA. No, it's okay.

SBONGILE. That was the new powerful poet on the block, Bonga Miya, giving us some of his ideas.

The band plays "Mka."

Scene 14

Jazz bar. Menzi is working through some chord progressions with the band when Bonga walks in. Menzi stops and confronts him.

MENZI. What's this rubbish you were saying on the radio?

BONGA. I was giving an honest reflection about everything and you call it rubbish?

MENZI. You say horrible things about me and you expect me to sit back and say you were "giving an honest reflection?" I made you, Bonga! You were nothing when you came to me. I took my time and built you up and today you reckon you are some smart poet?! You're running headlong into your doom. Mark my words.

BONGA. I'm sorry that I refuse to write like you. I took a path that's difficult, I know—standing against the likes of you. You refuse to tackle issues head-on in your writings and I don't think art is about that. On the radio I said that I think your writing is too safe and I still maintain that.

MENZI. What do you know about writing? What do you know about my writing?

BONGA. Not much, that I admit. But this much I know—that your writing is giving the right answers to the wrong questions. You once wrote about rape victims, an abortive attempt if I have to be honest. That piece was a sympathetic testament to rape victims. Nothing wrong with that. But have you ever thought about what makes black men rape their women? No, I don't think so. That's too close to home, it wouldn't go down well with your audiences in jazz clubs, no one would like you, there would be too much to lose. Dig the shit in the black man, that's where the healing lies—black men who rape their women. You think writing is fun, that it is being nice and coating words in caramel. It is a shit job! It is telling the truth even if it hurts. And it hurts all the way! The problem with this nation is the dick! Someone told us a terrible lie and we believed it. Someone told that us we have a big dick. Now we want to fuck everything that moves and we fuck ourselves in the process. (*Lady enters, carrying a traveling bag and looking very smart. Bonga is taken aback. To Menzi*) Oh, this is Lady. (*To Lady*) And this is Bro Menzi.

Menzi extends a hand, greets Lady, and offers her a seat. Bonga gets a drink and gives it to Lady. Menzi goes and stands next to the bar table.

LADY. Those were stupid things to say on the radio about black people.

BONGA. Someone had to say them.

LADY. You've made people angry.

BONGA. I know.

LADY. I hope you have the guts to stand for all you are doing.

BONGA. I hope so too.

LADY. Do you love me?

BONGA. Why do you want to know?

LADY. Because if you don't know you love me, how can you love me?

BONGA. Nobody is free.

LADY. What?

BONGA. You are asking me to answer questions of ultimate freedom.

LADY. What has freedom got to do with it? You speak big words but you can't answer one stupid question.

BONGA. Do you think that if I were free I would be here with you?

LADY. What did I ever do wrong that God punishes me so?

BONGA. The fact that I love you is an answer to itself. We can't know everything.

LADY. Why?

BONGA. Just the way it is.

LADY. I've decided to stop living with you. This is not the type of relationship I want to spend the rest of my life in. Not after years of trying and waiting for things to change for the better when, instead, they are getting worse by the day.

BONGA. I see.

LADY. Is that all you can say after all I have done for you?! After emptying my life into this relationship? You are so ungrateful.

BONGA. If you gave, you did because you wanted to. No one forces me to love you—I choose and I live with the consequences. Like everybody else, we try to face the harsh world together, side by side. And if it's not working for you, I understand. No one has it easy.

LADY. Why is it that everything is pain with you? You are not a writer. You are a destroyer. You destroy everything that comes into your life. You are incapable of being happy. You bring misery into people's lives! And you like it when they cannot take the pain you give them—you stand on the side and laugh while they struggle to live life according to your whims. You stand and enjoy when they die, broken and unhappy. I curse the day I met you.

BONGA. People don't need me to give them pain. The very fact of life is pain itself.

LADY. Yes, but people lead happy lives without knowing that. But once you cross their paths, all they see is gloom and sadness and they cannot enjoy their lives any more.

BONGA. The pain of dealing with the meaning of our lives is nothing compared to the pain of living with the darkness we carry in our hearts.

LADY. What about me, Bonga?

BONGA. What about you?

LADY. You promised me love . . . all I ever wanted was to have fun, but look at us?

BONGA. No one has fun, Lady. I used to believe that too. It's all an illusion and then we die. If you can't have fun with the sadness of your life, nobody will give it to you. (*Silence as Lady exits.*) Lady! (*She stops and turns to face him.*)

LADY. Menzi was right. You breathe hope and death in the same breath. (*Exits.*)

BONGA (*to Menzi*). Life's like that. We love it for healing us from its crushing wounds. (*Exits.*)

Scene 15

Lady and Bonga's apartment. Bonga is packing his bags when a knock is heard. He gets it and is met by a hail of bullets followed by a blackout and silence.

Scene 16

Jazz bar. Menzi under blue lights reciting a poem.

MENZI. Something deep within us is yearning
For things language cannot express for learning
Nor concoct words for meaning
No dirge can still its mourning

Something deep within us hungers
It never sleeps nor slumbers
But glares pitifully at these numbers
Us, as we live dangerously like mambas

Until we stop it will never flop
But rise it will to the top
Until the earth we lie atop
Reduced maybe to a pulp

Something deep within us is wanting
To want us to want it back
To it we are creatures that lack
For that, it never grows slack

The yearning is great
The hunger frightening
Who dares stop it?
It wants what it wants

End of Play

FROM LEFT TO RIGHT: *Mbulelo Grootboom (Solomon) and Aletta Bezuidenhout (Marion).*
Photograph by Frank Boye.

REACH

LARA FOOT NEWTON

Mbulelo Grootboom (Solomon). Photograph by Frank Boye.

CHARACTERS

MARION BANNING

63, South African with English heritage. She is solid, has her feet on the ground, a wry sense of humor, and an infinite need.

SOLOMON XABA

19, Rural Xhosa. He is inquisitive, aloof, and fragile—a hard shell with a baby center.

SETTING

Somewhere near Port Alfred, Eastern Cape, 2009—the year before the Football World Cup is to take place in South Africa—an event which South Africans see as the answer to all their transport, crime, and poverty issues.

A Victorian-style cottage.

The kitchen/lounge area.

The kitchen is warm and cozy.

Center upstage is the kitchen door.

The lounge is comfortable in a Victorian way. The furniture is worn and tired.

Family photographs line the walls.

There is a small writing desk downstage left.

There is a "wrap" around the stoep area.

Inspired by conversations with psychotherapist Tony Hamburger.

With gratitude to: Maurice Podbrey and the Mopo Cultural Trust.

Special thanks to: Lionel Newton, Liz Mills, Stefan Schmidtka (THEATER-FORMEN).

Reach was first produced by the Baxter Theatre Centre in 2007 for the THEATERFORMEN in Hanover.

MARION BANNING	Aletta Bezuidenhout
SOLOMON XABA	Mbulelo Grootboom
DIRECTOR	Clare Stopford
LIGHTING	Mannie Manim
SET DESIGN	Birrie le Roux

ACT I

A winter's night. The lights fade up on Marion Banning at the writing desk, a shawl covering her legs. She takes a deep drag on a cigarette, exhales, and picks up a pen . . .

MARION. My darling Anne (*She stops to smoke and think.*) Please forgive me, I know it has taken forever to write. I can't say that I have an excuse, except that the problems with the old ticker make me a little lethargic. Not that it has been bad, no pain at all, but let's just say that I am not quite as energetic as I used to be. (*Another puff*) You'll be pleased to hear that I have stopped smoking. I mean it would be silly to smoke with my condition, wouldn't it? (*Another puff*) Although it has improved of late . . . if the withdrawals are too much to bear, I might have the occasional puff . . . again . . . sometime. (*Puff*) Things are the same here, the mountain still cuts the sky in half, and it still has its many colors of orange, pink, purple, and gray. Still no rain, and still major power cuts.

The drought, I must tell you, is extreme. The air is thick with dust. And one feels thirsty all the time. Dry mouth, dry nose, dry eyes, dry everything!

I don't walk much any more, neither does anyone else it seems. Although a few weeks ago I did venture out. The paths through the forest where we used to walk Charlie and Shadow are quite empty now. (*Marion speaks the following lines without actually writing—a convention that should be used sporadically.*) No trace of families and picnics and kissing couples. I did however bump into Mr. Donavan. You remember him? The one with too much spit? And his dog, Fred. Why he doesn't put the poor thing out of its misery I'll never know. Three legs, blind, smelly! It can't possibly be . . . ?

On my way home, I came across a dead *mossie*[1] all covered in *goggas*.[2] It made me feel quite nauseous—why do they always have to do that?

---

1 Bird.
2 Maggots.

Do you remember that time when . . . (*The kitchen door opens tentatively behind her. She listens. A young black man sneaks in. He is wearing old but smart clothes. He is brooding, sullen. She senses his presence. Puts down her pen*) I have been waiting for you. (*Silence*) You have been lurking about my house for days now. If you are here to murder me, just hurry up and get on with it. I can't wait forever, you know. (*Slowly she turns to face the intruder*) And? What do you want? (*Pause*) Why didn't you knock? Where are your manners?

SOLOMON. I am Solomon Xaba.

MARION. Solomon?

SOLOMON. Yes, Mies[3] Marion, The grandchild of Thozama.

MARION. Thozama?

SOLOMON. Sandy—the lady who worked for . . .

MARION. Yes, yes. I know quite well who Thozama is, I just don't remember her having a grown-up grandson. My goodness! You're not little Solomon? Ha! You used to play in the fishpond while I pruned my icebergs. Terrorized the tadpoles! Captured them in jam jars.

SOLOMON. Yes.

MARION. What's the matter with you, anyway? I can't see you. Come closer. And shut the door. It's below zero, for fuck's sakes. (*He enters. Shiftily, he takes in the room. Edges forward into the light.*) Why are you so thin?

SOLOMON. It's the liver.

MARION. Yes dear, we all have one, but what's wrong with it?

SOLOMON (*tentative, unsure*). It's not working properly.

MARION. And neither is my fridge. What are you going to do about it? Have you been drinking lots of water? Vitamin B is very good, I believe.

SOLOMON. I went to the hospital.

MARION. And?

SOLOMON. They said I had one week to live. And they asked if I wanted to stay in hospital or die at home.

MARION. When was this?

SOLOMON. Last year.

---

3 Miss

MARION. So, quite clearly, you did neither.

SOLOMON. I went to see my aunt who is a *sangoma*. She gave me herbs from *Ikhala*,[4] and now I am better.

MARION. Well, good for you. I'm a great believer in herbs! Have you ever had your tea leaves read?

I should do it for you sometime! I'm very good, you know. Once, when reading my Aunt Martha's leaves, I saw a tall blonde standing next to a Mercedes Benz. Well, blow me down if six months later her husband didn't leave her for his blonde secretary. I'm not sure what she drove, but I can take a guess.

SOLOMON. Mercedes?

MARION. Bang on! Perhaps I should go and see your *sangoma* aunt, although it is probably too late now. I have heard that bay leaves are good for the heart, I wonder if there is any truth in that? It's always worth a try, but no. Too late now. I've given up, you see. Had enough! I may as well kill myself, but even that, my dear, takes too much energy for a Monday night. That's why I was rather hoping you would do it for me? Would you like a cigarette? (*She offers him one, he accepts but does not smoke.*) So! What are you doing here?

SOLOMON. My grandmother sent me, she says that you are sick. She says it is dangerous out here! You shouldn't be alone.

MARION. I haven't seen your grandmother in over two years! And I have been sick for nearly three. Anyway, its not like she lived here or anything—did the washing once a week that's all! I clean my own house, always have, don't need another woman to do it for me. So why the sudden concern?

He shrugs.

SOLOMON. *Andazi!*[5] She said I must look after you.

MARION. Well, I don't need any looking after. So off you go! Toodle doo! (*He does not move.*) Do you want money? Is that what this is about? (*She goes to the kitchen and takes some money from a tin*) It's all I have. (*Silence*) Do you want food? I'll make you a sandwich. (*She opens the broken, empty fridge*) Well, there's . . . butter? And if you are lucky . . . Ah yes, some bread. A little stale, but pre-blue! (*She makes the sandwich*) How is Thozama? (*Silence*) Such a powerful woman, as thin as a rake, but strong! Such determination. It's a won-

---

4 Aloe
5 I don't know!

der she didn't become president. What with her courage. But alas! We have had to put up with those awful men. All so full of their own spunk. And so conceited. (*She gives him the sandwich. He looks at it.*) The road to hell is paved with men with ill intentions, or even worse—no intentions at all. Wouldn't you agree?

Silence. He wraps the sandwich in some paper and puts it carefully into his pocket.

SOLOMON. Thank you for the sandwich. (*He makes to go.*)

MARION. Will you come again?

SOLOMON. What for?

MARION. I have no idea. (*He exits, closes the door. She goes back to her writing desk. Picks up her pen*) You'll never guess who just popped in? Do you remember little Solomon? I always thought he might amount to something, such intelligent eyes. Remember his grandmother, Sandy? She and I used to smoke secretly together on the back porch. Your father would have murdered me if he had found out. He was always so bally self-righteous, I suppose academics always are.

Maybe it's a good thing you married an accountant, they may be . . . quiet, but not quite so arrogant.

I'm reading Coetzee's *Slow Man*—better late than never. If you ever come across him in Australia, give him a kick from me would you? What is it with him? The most depressing piece of literature ever conceived of—it makes *Disgrace* read like a fairy tale . . .

Do you think I might have been nicer to your father? I sometimes imagine that things could have been better, perhaps if I had . . . (*looking up*) reached out a little . . .

(*Transition. Music. Lights. Marion is sitting at the kitchen table drinking a cup of tea. Sunlight streams through the window. The door opens. No one appears*) You again. I told you to knock! Now close the door and try again! (*The door closes. There is a knock*) Come in! (*Nothing*) Come in! (*Nothing. She stands, and opens the door. There is no one there! She bends down and picks up a Checkers packet. She looks inside. She sticks her hand into the bag and pulls out some chicken feet. She looks at the feet, disgusted. She puts them back in the packet. Throws the packet out the door, and slams it shut! Washes her hands. She sits at the table. Silence. Lights a cigarette. She picks up* Slow Man *and reads a bit.*) Oh, for God's sake!

(*Transition. Music. Lights up. Marion sits at her desk.*) My darling, it is taking me forever to finish this letter. I keep losing my train of thought.

Tell me, how are the boys? Michael must be getting to be a big boy now? And how is Peter's pencil grip? You must sort that out. You don't want him lagging behind.

Bad handwriting is a sign of slothfulness, and our Peter is not a sloth. Now I'm not interfering, just doing my duty as a grandmother. And please watch that Australian drawl, it really isn't an attractive accent. When I spoke to him on his birthday, I could barely understand a word he said. Not that I am criticizing you as a mother—on the contrary, you are a brilliant mother, but there are things a grandmother can see that a mother can't.

I'm sure that you are not the least bit . . . (*There is a knock at the door. She gets up quietly and tiptoes to the door. She opens it suddenly*) Ha! Got you! (*She chuckles*) Well, come in if you must. (*Solomon follows her in*) What was the meaning of those disgusting feet? Explain yourself, young man!

SOLOMON. *Amanqina.*

MARION. Chicken feet.

SOLOMON. Yes. You had no food in your house. My grandmother says you must eat.

MARION. Your grandmother must be going quite dotty, my boy. She knows very well that I would never eat chicken feet. Liver, yes! Pope's nose? Perhaps. But not feet.

SOLOMON. Pope's nose?

MARION. The rear end.

SOLOMON. The gat?[6]

MARION. I suppose.

SOLOMON. What did you do with the feet?

MARION. What does one usually do with chicken feet, my dear? Throw them away. You didn't really expect me to eat them, did you? There is a certain point, my boy, at which cultures will never coincide. My line in the sand is chicken feet. What's yours?

SOLOMON. I could have cooked them for you.

---

6 The bum?

MARION. You could have smoked them for me, and marinated them in champagne for all I care. I still would not have eaten them. Surely, you see my point. There must be a few things that you would refuse to eat, that us English regard as a delicacy—pigs' testicles for instance?

Silence.

SOLOMON. Really? You eat pigs' testicles?

MARION. Just pulling your leg. We might be eccentric, but we are not that bad. Although us English are mere facilitators now, here in South Africa, I mean. We no longer participate. Not so?

SOLOMON. I once ate the eye of a cat.

MARION. Really?

SOLOMON (*laughs*). We might be savage but we are not that bad.

MARION. My goodness. A sense of humor! That's a luck! Would you like to have some tea with me? (*Silence*) Now tell me, my boy, have you finished school?

SOLOMON. Yes.

MARION. And what about university?

SOLOMON. I don't think so.

MARION. And a job?

SOLOMON. Not a real one. But I do some odd jobs. I can paint your house if you want me to.

MARION. I'd prefer you to further your education.

SOLOMON. There are no jobs anyway. Unemployment has never been higher.

She gives him tea in a delicate teacup and saucer.

MARION. An education is not about employment. An education is about being educated.

SOLOMON. Maybe you can educate me?

MARION. I'm not qualified. All I am really is a housewife—mother, gardener, and avid reader.

I have tried my hand at poetry, and was even published once. But I'm not a professional anything. A degree in sociology, mind you. But that was donkey's years ago.

I'm afraid I have no milk. Or sugar.

SOLOMON. I thought all white people had groceries.

MARION (*laughs*). When you live alone, the inclination to shop and cook begins to dwindle. There's no point, really. Besides, I have been ill. Not much of an appetite.

SOLOMON. Where is your daughter?

MARION. Anne? She's in Australia. Married to a boring accountant. Two lovely boys and a nice home in a nice leafy suburb.

SOLOMON. Have you visited her?

MARION. No. They used to come here every second year. But not since the country has . . . become so violent. They're too nervous.

SOLOMON. And you? Are you not nervous?

MARION. One is only nervous if one has something to lose. It's a pathology really, fear. The world bought into it a hundred years ago.

Do you know, I think I might still have some Matzas and Marmite. My favorite! I've suddenly developed a little hunger.

SOLOMON. Are you not scared of dying here alone? Maybe you should go live with your daughter.

MARION. Maybe you should mind your own beeswax.

Do you really think I want to die in Australia? Ah . . . "the horror, the horror." It would mean that my life had been worth absolutely nothing. (*Pause*) At least, here I have my memories. Jolly good ones. Do you think I want to rot in Australian earth? My God, I can think of nothing lonelier, more frightening . . . Australian worms and maggots.

My life has been full here. Painful but full!

Try one? (*Giving him a Matza.*)

SOLOMON. And now? . . . Your life?

MARION. Well, now . . . it is empty, but once, not that long ago I had a full life. A husband that I tolerated and sometimes loved. A daughter who perhaps doesn't like me that much, but nevertheless is my daughter, and a son who I . . . idolized. That's quite rich, don't you think, that accounts for at least a little. I have seen this country through good and bad and good and bad. I was even a little involved in the struggle. Not bravely so, but involved. The struggle—isn't that a haphazard sort of term?—the struggle—as if it was finite. With a beginning and an end. How I wish that that were the case.

But I suppose you weren't even alive in those days. When were you born?

SOLOMON. 1990. I'll be 20 next year in 2010.

MARION. So you missed most of it . . . Or have you?

SOLOMON. I think you should leave. I think it is not safe for you here. This land is . . . there is fighting. Protests. They are talking about giving it back to its real owners.

MARION. Real owners? I'm not even sure that one can own land. A history? Maybe. A past? Certainly. But land. That's different.

I know about all this stuff. The government has already made me an offer. It's not that I believe they shouldn't have it, you understand? It's just— where would I go? They must hang on for a while . . . a few more years at most.

SOLOMON. Here. You are in-between. It is not safe.

MARION. In-between?

SOLOMON. You are not in town.

MARION. No.

SOLOMON. And you are not in the township.

MARION. Thus I am in-between?

SOLOMON. You must write to your daughter and tell her you are coming.

MARION. Have you not heard a single thing I have said? Listen to me, my boy, this is my home. I was born here, and I intend to die here!

SOLOMON. Yes, you were born here. But you are a racist like the rest of them.

MARION. Me? Racist?

SOLOMON. All the time, you call me "my boy" just like your father called my father.

MARION. Oh for fuck's sake! "My boy" is not only a racist term. "My boy," is what I called my son. "My boy" can just as well be a term of endearment.

SOLOMON. Endearment?

MARION. Of care. Of caring.

SOLOMON. Are you saying that you care for me?

MARION. I'm not sure what I'm saying. I think you should go now, I'm feeling quite exhausted.

SOLOMON. *Nyana wam.* "My boy." It's what my grandmother called me when she was alive.

MARION. When she was alive?

SOLOMON. She died a year ago. TB.

MARION. What are you saying? What are you playing at? You said your grandmother sent you here to look after me.

SOLOMON. It's true. I was sent here. But not by my grandmother.

MARION. Then by whom?

SOLOMON. It doesn't matter.

MARION. Look, I don't like these games. What do want? Just get out of here. You're upsetting me. Go away! Please, you're disturbing me. Leave. Please.

Silence. He does not move.

SOLOMON (*threatening*). This place is lonely. (*Pause*) It is blind, it is deaf, it doesn't see. Someone could kill you and no one would hear. (*Looking around*) You don't even lock the doors, there are no burglar bars. Not even an old black dog to keep you company.

Silence.

MARION. It's time you left. (*Silence. Solomon exits, the door closes. She lights a smoke, goes to the cupboard, and takes some tablets. She sits at her writing desk. Picks up the pen but doesn't write.*) At least, if it were violent one might put up a fight. Show some life.

There it is again, that stuck feeling. A paralysis. Like being bitten by a snake.

One waits for that thing to happen. But what thing? What if dear Sisyphus had made it, and the rock had rolled over the other side? And there was just another mountain?

It all seems so pointless. (*She begins to write*) Perhaps if I had given Jonathan and Dad more space, your father would not have felt so isolated. You never know, he might even have been able to be a bit stronger, to hold me a little. Sometimes isolation is not only about geography. A great big cavity.

Transition. Mandoza music.[7] Lights up on Solomon. He is carrying a small CD player and a ladder. He puts both down, sets up the ladder, goes outside, fetches a

---

7 Well known as Mandoza, Mduduzi Tshabalala Minsimang (1978–) is a South African kwaito musician.

tin of paint and brush. Pours paint into a pan, climbs the ladder, and begins to paint the wall. Enjoying the music. Marion enters, wearing a dressing gown. Sees Solomon, lights a cigarette, sits down on the couch, and watches him.

SOLOMON. Morning, Mies. I'm here to paint your house. There is some *mngqusho*[8] on the stove. You must eat.

She gets up, looks at the pot on the stove, gives it a stir.

MARION (*above the music*). You still haven't told me what you are doing here?

SOLOMON. What?

Marion turns the music off.

MARION. What a terrible sound!

SOLOMON. Mandoza! The king!

MARION. You still haven't told me what you are doing here.

SOLOMON. I told you, I have come to paint your house.

MARION. Well, I'm not paying you a penny.

SOLOMON. I didn't ask for a penny.

MARION. Where did you get the paint?

SOLOMON. Hardware.

MARION. How much did it cost?

SOLOMON. Nothing. (*Laughs.*)

MARION. You stole it?

SOLOMON. I just borrowed it. (*Laughing*) I'll take the tin back tomorrow.

MARION. Well, at least you borrowed a tasteful color.

SOLOMON (*looking at the tin*). Rice paper! (*Laughing and shaking his head*) *Umlungus!*[9]

MARION. That tickles you does it? Rice paper?

He laughs more.

SOLOMON. If it was called white or cream, it would cost half.

MARION. Yes, but it wouldn't be rice paper. How did you choose it?

---

8 Samp or mixed beans.
9 White people!

SOLOMON. I just chose the most expensive one. That's how white people choose, isn't it?

MARION. No, definitely not! I've always been very frugal. I had to be, my husband was a miser.

SOLOMON. Do you know grated cheese?

MARION. Yes, of course I do. I brought both my children up on it. At one stage it was all Jonathan would eat.

SOLOMON. After I finished school I went to the city, I worked as a packer at Woolworth's—it was a good job, I saved a lot of money.

Do you know how much it is for grated cheese at Woolworth's?

MARION. No. I grate my own. But I must say it is quite a mission, especially if you are making macaroni.

SOLOMON. Twenty-seven rands a packet! The same cheese in a block costs 19 rand.

MARION. Honestly? That's ridiculous!

SOLOMON. What's more ridiculous is that at the Sparza where I live, you can get the same cheese for four rands.

MARION. The exact same cheese?

SOLOMON. Exact!

MARION. Daylight robbery!

SOLOMON. And chickens? What makes a Woolworth's chicken so special? Are Woolworth's chickens any different from Sparza chickens? Do Woolworth's chickens get fed condensed milk and . . . *boerewors*[10] when they are babies? No! They get *miel*,[11] like all the other chickens! Are they slagged with a golden knife? No, they are slagged like all the other chickens! But a Woolworth's chicken is 49 rand!

MARION. Honestly, is that what they cost nowadays?

SOLOMON. A Sparza chicken is 12 rand! Now, where's the other 30-something rand?

MARION. No idea! But that sounds like a decent job. Why did you leave?

---

10 Traditional South African sausage roll, usually barbequed.
11 Maize meal/corn.

SOLOMON. Fired!

MARION. Why? Did you borrow a chicken?

SOLOMON. Never, I don't steal from people who I work for.

MARION. So, why were you fired?

SOLOMON. There was this one *mlungu*[12] woman, she says to me, "Excuse me, where is the Hollandaise source?" And I say, " I don't know, Madam" and then she says, "Well, do you work here or not?"

"I do Madam." Then her cellphone rings, she answers it and she says. "Hi, just hold on, I'm in Woolworth's and they're telling me there is no Hollandaise sauce I tell you this country is going down the drain I'll phone you back soon."

"Where is your manager?" she asks me. But I don't want her to call the manager, so I say, "I don't think we have Hollands sauce Madam, but we have a special on barbeque sauce!" (*Marion laughs*) "Are you trying to be funny? You want me to get you fired?"

"No Madam, please." Then I look in her trolley and I see three chickens. Then I say, "You know Madam, just 10 minutes down the road at my Sparza, you can get chickens for 12 rands, if the Madam can wait till one o'clock— I can take you there!" (*Marion laughs.*)

MARION. You didn't!

SOLOMON. I think I did it on purpose. I was unhappy there. Smiling at everyone, just like a clown. She spoke to the manager, she said I was being cheeky and I was fired the same day!

MARION (*still laughing*). Hollandaise sauce—I've always thought it overrated.

SOLOMON. My favorite job I ever had was here at Feathers.

MARION. The chicken farm?

SOLOMON. Yes.

MARION. What is it with you and chickens?

SOLOMON. There I worked with the eggs. I would sit in a small dark room with a special light. I would shine the light under the egg and then I could see right inside. The eggs with a red blob, I would put to one side. The others—

---

12 . . . white . . .

large and medium—separate—and then they would be delivered to the shops.

MARION. And you liked that job?

SOLOMON. Very much. Sometimes I would feel sorry for the eggs that had the blobs inside, and then I would let one or two go through. But not often.

MARION. The specially chosen?

SOLOMON. Yes.

MARION. Like God!

SOLOMON. Yes.

MARION. Do you believe in God?

SOLOMON. What else? (*He climbs down from the ladder and goes to the kitchen. Dishes up some food.*) Where is your TV?

MARION. In the garage and broken. I don't watch any more. All a load of bollocks! No television and no newspapers that's my promise to myself. Why hammer more nails into the coffin if you don't need to?

SOLOMON. Next year is the World Cup! You have to get a television.

MARION. I don't like soccer! Makes no sense. Never has. Lots of men kicking a ball—back and forth, back and forth—like mindless animals. The crowd going bananas, for no reason at all! Acting like hooligans! Stampedes, fistfights. It's barbaric!

SOLOMON. You must learn the rules. Then you will know what's going on. I will get you a television, and then I will teach you. You'll like it, you'll see!

MARION. There will be no television in my house, Solomon, over my dead body.

SOLOMON. Which will not be very long if you carry on smoking so much.

MARION. Now don't you start! My one small pleasure in life. Tell me, Solomon, how much do cigarettes cost at your Sparza?

SOLOMON. I'm not buying you cigarettes! You don't need them.

MARION. Talking of the garage—it is full of junk that you might find useful. Old clothes, the kids' bicycles, at least two lawnmowers. You should help yourself. You might be able to use some of it. Or sell it if you like.

SOLOMON. I'll have a look. Thank you. (*He gives her a bowl of* mngqusho. *She takes it.*)

MARION. I remember this, Thozama used to make it for my kids.

SOLOMON. *Mngqusho.*

MARION. *Mngq . . . Mngq*

SOLOMON. *Mngqusho.*

MARION. *Mngqusho.*

SOLOMON. Very good.

MARION. So Thozama passed away?

SOLOMON. Yes.

MARION. I'm sorry to hear it. Was it an easy death? Did she struggle, or suffer?

SOLOMON. She died . . . for a long time.

MARION. Oh. And what happened to your parents, Solomon? Where is your mother?

SOLOMON. They both died when I was 10.

MARION. Both? In the same year?

SOLOMON. My father, 26 February, and my mother, 17 November. But my father did not stay with us—only at the end.

MARION. Tragedy. What did they die of?

SOLOMON (*shrugs*). We are not sure. They got very sick. Like cattle in the drought. The people in our village were all gossiping—they said it was AIDS. Some would not come near our house.

MARION. That fucking AIDS! God's sick sense of humor. Why is it that tragedy always strikes the poorer areas? Think about it—earthquakes, tsunamis, disease—always in areas where people are already struggling to survive. Why can't a tsunami hit the White House, for instance? Okay, so there is no sea in the vicinity, but you get my point? When I do finally kick the bucket, I'm going to have a word with God about his selection process! Clearly, it needs to be updated! A little re-distribution if you please.

I mean how can a child lose both its parents in the same year? Where is the justice in that?

Solomon scrapes the rest of the mngqusho *carefully into a packet and ties a knot.*

SOLOMON. It sucks!

MARION. It what?

SOLOMON. Sucks!

MARION. Yes I suppose it does, but, for fuck's sake, choose a better word my boy—"sucks" is hardly English.

SOLOMON. What should I say then?

MARION (*thinking*). Ah . . . it . . . I suppose sucks will do. And so your grandmother took care of you?

SOLOMON. Yes, we were the lucky ones. Some of the other kids didn't have grandparents. At school, they shouted at me and chased me with sticks. One teacher even said I was not allowed in the classroom. But then my grandmother went and spoke to him. She said that if I was chased from school she would report the school to the police and that every child had the right to education. The teacher let me back in the class but I had to sit on my own, next to the window. I didn't care, I hated his class anyway. Mathematics! Ga!

MARION. I remember Thozama saying that her daughter was ill. At one stage she asked if she could borrow money.

SOLOMON. Did you give it to her?

MARION. No. I never lent money to anyone. It was my policy.

But had I known that things were so bad at home I'm sure I would have. Or, at least, I like to think I would have. Strange how one sets principles, lives by them, and then later one realizes that ones principles are worth nothing in the light of reality. (*Silence*) I think I need a little nap.

SOLOMON. Yes. You always sleep at this time. Wake up in the morning, drink tea, and then sleep on the couch. Two or three hours. Wake up, sit for a long time, looking at nothing. Then read, without really looking. More tea, more cigarettes, then sleep. Then the sun goes down. Dark comes.

More tea, and then write. Sit at your desk for a long time, staring at nothing.

MARION. So you really have been spying on me?

SOLOMON. No. Just watching you.

MARION. For how long?

SOLOMON. Long time.

MARION. How long?

SOLOMON. Some years.

MARION. Some years!

SOLOMON. Maybe.

MARION. What on earth for?

SOLOMON. I don't know.

MARION. Was it your grandmother who sent you? Or is it those protestors? The ones who want my land. Have they put you up to this?

SOLOMON. No.

MARION. Maybe you are painting the house for them?

SOLOMON. No.

MARION. Then they can have the rice-paper house.

SOLOMON. No.

MARION. What else have you seen me do?

SOLOMON. Not much. I saw you go for a walk the other day. I saw you throw a brick at a dead bird.

MARION. It wasn't at the bird, it was at the maggots.

SOLOMON. You threw a brick at maggots?

MARION. Yes.

SOLOMON. And then you cried. For a long time. Put your behind on the ground and cried like a wildebeest.

MARION. I don't like maggots . . . What else have you seen me do? Do you watch me on the toilet? In the shower? What about my privacy?

SOLOMON. I've seen you sitting on your bed and looking at nothing, sometimes for the whole night.

My grandmother used to do that. What are you thinking about?

MARION. Well, at least I can keep that private.

I think you should go now Solomon, you're making me uncomfortable.

SOLOMON. Like you, I have nothing to lose. (*Carries on painting. Silence, she looks at him*) Do you want me to fetch your book? Do you want to read?

MARION. No. I hate my book.

SOLOMON. What is it about.

MARION. A man with one leg who wants sex.

SOLOMON. Is that all?

MARION. A lonely man. Visited by a strange woman.

ABOVE: *Mbulelo Grootboom (Solomon, standing) and Aletta Bezuidenhout (Marion, lying).*
BELOW, FROM LEFT TO RIGHT: *Aletta Bezuidenhout (Marion) and Mbulelo Grootboom (Solomon).*
Photographs by Frank Boye.

ABOVE: *Aletta Bezuidenhout* (*Marion*).

BELOW, FROM LEFT TO RIGHT: *Aletta Bezuidenhout* (*Marion*), *Mbulelo Grootboom* (*Solomon*). *Photographs by Frank Boye*.

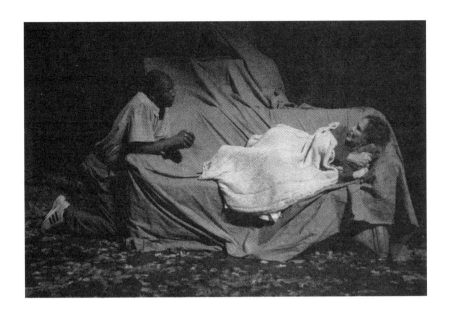

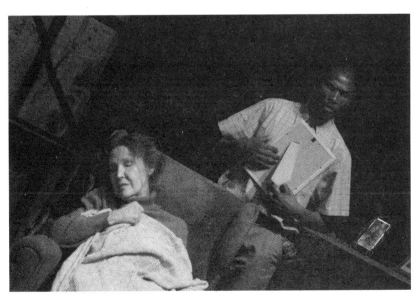

ABOVE, FROM LEFT TO RIGHT: *Mbulelo Grootboom (Solomon), Aletta Bezuidenhout (Marion).*
BELOW: *Aletta Bezuidenhout (Marion, sitting), Mbulelo Grootboom (Solomon, standing).*
Photographs by Frank Boye.

SOLOMON. Sounds boring.

MARION. Yes, it is.

SOLOMON. I will bring you some interesting books.

MARION. You?

SOLOMON. Me! I have plenty.

MARION. Who are you, Solomon?

SOLOMON. When I was younger, I helped older boys from the gangs to steal. I would pretend that I was begging in town—then I would stand close to a autobank machine and remember the secret number. Then I would tell the older boys and they would give me five rands.

MARION. And then? What would they do?

SOLOMON. I don't know. I don't do it any more. Now I help the other kids. The ones like me.

MARION. How do you mean?

SOLOMON. There is a safe place for children near where I live. It's run by Ma'am Gladys. She looks after 29 children. Sometimes I take them sweets. Other times food, and, if I have nothing, I tell them a story.

MARION. You read to them?

SOLOMON. No, I just tell it to them. Bible stories or ones that my mother told me. Or ones I remember from my dreams.

MARION. That's kind of you. You should tell me one sometime.

SOLOMON. Maybe. Sometime I will tell you the story about the invisible monkey, it is my favorite.

MARION. All right.

Solomon points to one of the pictures on the wall.

SOLOMON. Your daughter?

MARION. Yes. Anne. Pretty, don't you think?

SOLOMON. Very! (*He dusts the picture and takes it down.*)

MARION. And those are my grandchildren—little horrors. Michael, the one in red, is a genius. Sensitive boy with a wonderful sense of humor—takes after me, of course!

SOLOMON. And this one?

MARION. Peter. Just like his mother—bullish, aggressive but with a big heart— Neither are like their father. Thank goodness for small blessings! (*He begins to take the other portraits off the wall so that he can paint.*) Not that one. I think, leave that one there. It's not really necessary to take it down, is it?

SOLOMON. This is Jonathan?

MARION. Yes.

SOLOMON. Okay. I will paint around him. Can I turn the music back on? Just very softly?

MARION. All right. If you must. (*He turns it on, and continues to paint. She continues to eat, occasionally allowing her head to bob in time to the music. Cross fade to later in the day as he continues to paint.*)

I wonder if my Jonathan would have liked this music. Probably—he was completely tone deaf and color blind, poor boy. Once, when he was very small, we had two family cats—a ginger one and a black one. I was at my desk writing and he came into the room and said, "Mom, the cat ate my tooth." I didn't even know that he had lost a tooth. And so I said, "Well where did you put it my boy?"

And he said, "In my slipper."

"Do you know which cat it was?" I asked.

"The green one," he said. (*She chuckles*) To this day I don't know if it was the ginger or the black.

He was a good boy, my Jonathan. I always wished I could see through his eyes for a little while, just to see what his world looked like. (*She dozes off.*)

Solomon watches Marion quietly. He stops to look at the picture of Jonathan. He makes sure that Marion is not watching. He sits on top of the ladder, takes the picture off the wall and looks at it carefully. Transition. Music.

Possible End of Act I

ACT II

Lights up. Solomon is asleep on the couch! Marion enters in her gown.

MARION. Rise and shine! There is work to be done—you can't leave my house half-painted.

SOLOMON (*wakes and stretches*). I need food.

MARION. I think there is bread.

SOLOMON. I need meat. Meat and *atcha*![13]

MARION. For breakfast? You'll give yourself an ulcer. (*Looking in the cupboard*) There's baked beans.

SOLOMON. Great! (*She opens a tin and puts it on a plate. He goes outside.*) I must six nine.[14]

MARION. Whatever. (*Solomon returns and takes the plate. She dabbles with the paint-brush and begins to paint. He laughs at the sight.*) What? (*He laughs some more.*)

SOLOMON. You look funny!

MARION. Funny ha-ha? Or funny peculiar?

SOLOMON. Funny ha-ha!

MARION. Thanks.

SOLOMON. An old white woman, in her nightgown, with a paintbrush and a cigarette!

MARION. I'm not that old! And don't think I can't paint. I painted this whole house some 20 years ago. All on my own. Did a good job too.

SOLOMON. You should come to the township and paint my grandmother's house. It needs a bit of attention.

MARION. Well, if you borrow some more paint, I might take you up on it. Do you pay well?

SOLOMON. Very well! You missed a spot there!

MARION (*getting tired*). Okay, that's me for today! You had better take over.

SOLOMON. These workers of today! Lazy! And expensive!

MARION. You really should try and get a proper job, Solomon. You can't simply walk into someone's house and start painting it. Have you looked in the classifieds? You're a clever boy—there must be something. This is the old—new South Africa. What about all that "affirmative action" stuff?

SOLOMON. This is the Cape, Mies Marion. Here, the Europeans are still . . .

---

13 . . . curry.

14 I must piss.

MARION. Still what?

SOLOMON. Still European.

MARION. Yes, that's true enough. But should that stop you?

SOLOMON. No. It's not what stops me.

MARION. Then what is it?

SOLOMON. Maybe I'm afraid.

MARION. You?

SOLOMON. If I get a proper job, I will have to move to the city. I will have to leave my house and stay in a shack, where people live on top of each other like cockroaches. I did go there once, but only for a few months. I got a job very quickly first at Woolworths, then as a griller in a restaurant. But I was very unhappy. At night, I slept with my eyes wide open like an owl because I was scared that someone was going to kill me. None of the girls were interested in me because I didn't have fancy clothes, and the other men were always taking my money and never giving it back. I missed my grandmother, and my little sister. I took my last pay and bought a bus-ticket home.

MARION. Poor Solomon. Just a simple farm boy at heart. And there I thought you were one of those awful tsotsiies. (*She sits down at her desk . . . Transition. Music.*) No, I haven't posted it yet. Well, at least it will be a nice long one.

Solomon has been visiting regularly, painting the house and chatting away. Nice boy. At first I was suspicious. What was he doing here? What did he want? But now I think that he, like me, just needs a little company. We talk a lot, listen to music. I have even taught him to play scrabble.

Do you know that next week is the anniversary? Seven years. Can you believe it Anne?

Seven years. It seems like just yesterday. But let me not get too morbid.

Spring is in the air. I'm thinking of planting a few bulbs. I've neglected the garden over the last few years, but, now that I have Solomon, I was thinking that he could help me.

No good having a pretty garden if you can't share it with someone.

Solomon enters—he is wearing a yellow shirt. He carries garden shears. Marion is startled.

SOLOMON. Mies Marion, I found all the garden equipment. Spades, picks, everything! They were under the old canopy.

MARION. Where did you get that shirt?

SOLOMON. I found it in the boxes in the garage.

MARION. Take it off!!

SOLOMON. What? I . . .

MARION. Take it off!!!!!!!!!!!!!! (*Solomon unbuttons the shirt*) How dare you! You think you can come into my house and fucking well take over my life. Fucking well wear my son's clothes. Who the hell do you think you are?

SOLOMON (*drops the shirt*). Mies Marion, I'm sorry I thought you said . . .

MARION. You thought nothing!!!!!!!!! (*She picks up the shirt*) This is my shirt!! My Jonathan's shirt and now you've gone and ruined it. Made it dirty. It's filthy, it's . . . it's . . . oh my God it's nearly seven years. Seven years without my boy . . .

SOLOMON (*shaken*). Mies Marion, I didn't . . . I'm sorry . . . I'll go now. (*He doesn't move*) Mies Marion . . .

MARION. Please don't go Solomon. It's not your fault. I . . . Oh God, of course you can have the shirt. Of course you can wear it. I just . . . I just got a fright. For an instant I saw Jonathan . . . I bought him this shirt for his graduation, I remember it well—I wanted him to wear a crisp, white shirt but he refused. He wanted something bright, something different.

Solomon sits down next to her.

SOLOMON. Mies Marion . . . (*he begins to cry.*)

MARION. Please put it on. Put it on . . . it looks very nice on you.

SOLOMON. No, it's okay.

MARION. Please. (*She picks it up and starts to dress him—intimate in an uncomfortable way*) There, there. Look at you. Look how wonderful you look. (*He leans his head against her shoulder. Tentatively she puts an arm round him for comfort. He sobs*) It's okay my boy, I'm sorry, I'm so sorry . . . sh . . . sh . . . shhhhh— (*She rocks him back and forth; he calms down*) I have an idea! Why don't you tell me that story, your favorite . . . the one about the invisible monkey.

SOLOMON. Now?

MARION. Yes. It will cheer us both up.

SOLOMON. I will tell you the dream.

MARION. Okay.

SOLOMON. I dream I am my shadow, in a big, still water in the river.

MARION. Your reflection?

SOLOMON. That's right.

> I am a small boy and I like to wave at my reflection. Then, one day, my reflection calls me, "Hey *chomie*!¹⁵ Come inside!" So I get inside—to my shadow—and I feel very safe, safe from the wind, safe from the *ouens*,¹⁶ safe from the disease that killed my mother.

> I feel warm, but, when I look in the mirror, I cannot see myself.

MARION. And then?

SOLOMON. Nothing!

MARION. You wake up?

SOLOMON. I think so.

MARION. I sometimes dream that all my teeth fall out! Just like that! In one go, like peanuts.

SOLOMON (*giggling*). That's terrible.

MARION. Now what on earth could that mean? (*They chuckle. Transition. Music. Lights up on Marion writing.*)

> I'm cooking a lamb stew for tonight, remember the one with peas that you love so much? It's a surprise for Solomon. He is always complaining that there is no food in the house. So I phoned, Mr. Wilson and he made a delivery. Vegetables, meat, the works. I may even open a bottle of wine, I still have some that your father left here. Is it true that red wine doesn't go off? Well, I suppose we can only but try.

> Did I tell you that we had a tiny bit of rain last week? Just a drizzle but better than nothing . . . small drops on acres of dust.

> (*There is a knock. Solomon enters*) Ah! At last you have learned to knock! Come in Solomon, give that pot a stir will you? I'm just finishing off this letter.

> *She continues to write.*

SOLOMON. This smells delicious!

MARION. I thought I'd make something special for a change.

---

15 "Hey friend! . . ."
16 . . . boys, . . .

SOLOMON. Mmm. I thought you just ate Matzas. When can we eat? I'm starving.

MARION. Half an hour or so. The secret with lamb is to cook it slowly. I've made some Yorkshire pudding to go with it. Used to be Jonathan's favorite.

SOLOMON. Mmm. I like pudding. Do you know that my grandmother once cooked and ate a moose?

MARION. A moose? Nonsense!

SOLOMON. I'm telling you. Once there were two mooses that ran through the village of Oxtin.

MARION. Two mooses? One moose, two mooses? Mice? Meese? Meeses? Anyway whatever! It is impossible—there are no moose in South Africa.

SOLOMON. Once there were two. My grandmother was 13 at the time and very hungry because she was pregnant with my mother. Then, one day, there was chaos in the village—a strange beast had been spotted running through the streets. My grandmother and some boys and some dogs chased it for a long time and then got it stuck up against a fence. Then they threw rocks at it till it was dead. They divided the meat, and my grandmother took a leg home with her to cook. Her mother, my great grandmother, shouted at her, "Take that foreign beast from the house! You can't cook that here, the ancestors will be angry with you!" But my grandmother just answered, "*Ag* man! The ancestors are already angry." Then she made a big fire and cooked the beast. She said it tasted delicious.

MARION. But what was a moose doing in Oxtin?

SOLOMON. Some said that the mooses, were being transported to the zoo and that the truck had had an accident on the highway.

MARION. And was that true?

SOLOMON. I think so, because the next day the police came to my grandmother's mother's house. They were looking for the hide of the animal. They said that my grandmother was in trouble, because it had been a gift from the Swedish ambassador to the zoo of the Eastern Cape.

MARION. And what did your grandmother say?

SOLOMON. She pretended that the baby was coming, and began to scream. Then the police left.

MARION. My goodness. That Thozama! What a woman. A moose in the Karoo! I think we can probably eat now—it should be ready. Would you like to open that bottle of wine? Courtesy of my husband. Either he forgot about his stash in the pantry. Or it's no good. Either way, let's give it a try.

SOLOMON (*looking at the bottle*). I think it must be *vrot*[17]—1999?

MARION. Well, wine is supposed to get better with age. Although they say it doesn't keep forever.

He opens it and pours two glasses.

SOLOMON. You never talk much about your husband. Are you divorced?

MARION. Yes, six years ago. After . . . Jonathan, there was no reason to stay together. We couldn't bear to even look at each other any more. It's a shame, he wasn't a bad husband, old Frank, but he was always quite a weak man. A raging hypochondriac, a miser, and at times a bit of a fool. But he was the provider and he did take his part very seriously. (*She gives him a plate of food. Raises her glass*) Cheers! Mmm, not bad!

My favorite story about old Frank, one which I used to tell with relish whenever I got the chance, much to his disapproval . . . What's the stew like?

SOLOMON. The best I have ever tasted.

MARION. Good. . . . is the story about the night he was close to death. He woke me up in the middle of the night screaming in agony. "Marion, Marion, I'm dying!"

Well, I turned the light on and there he was sweating, crying, and looking quite blue.

"Ah the pain!!!!" He said. "It's cutting through my belly like a knife, I feel like I've been poisoned."

I was quite concerned—we tried the warm tea and the Buscopan and whatever else I had in the house, and finally ended up calling the ambulance. (*Laughs.*)

On the way to the hospital he thanked me for all the wonderful years. And for being a beautiful mother and a kind wife—we were both in tears. I remembered all the good things about him—the day Anne was born and he bought me three dozen red roses, and the holiday when Jonathan was stung by a bluebottle and Frank picked him up and ran all the way up the hill and over the bridge to the hotel.

---

17 . . . bad—

Then we arrived at the hospital and there was this young fat intern doctor on duty.

Frank insists on ICU and specialists. But the intern says that he needs to first give Frank an examination. (*Laughs more.*)

So he prods Frank's stomach, here, there, and everywhere and suddenly (*laughing so much she can hardly speak*) Frank lets out this godawful fart! The longest fart in the history of civilization!

SOLOMON (*laughs*). *Ya Suza?*[18]

MARION. The best was his face when he heard the sound. A wonderful mixture of disbelief, shock, and embarrassment!

SOLOMON (*laughing*). And the pain was gone?

MARION. In a puff! (*Still laughing*) Needless to say, he hated it when I told the story! Which I did, whenever I had too much to drink. This wine is good!

Silence.

SOLOMON. I was there when Jonathan was killed.

Silence. Marion, is overwhelmed, she cannot speak. Then . . .

MARION. You knew Jonathan?

SOLOMON. He often bought me sweets . . .

MARION. . . . He came home for the vacation . . .

SOLOMON. . . . I was playing in the veld nearby . . .

MARION. . . . It was at my insistence that Anne and her family had driven down from Jo'burg for Christmas and I wanted the family together . . . (*She becomes quiet, looking at him—full of light for the truth . . .*)

SOLOMON. I saw Douglass, Sticks, and Arthur—these were boys that my grandmother said I should never speak to, but they were walking with Jonathan to the scrapyard and so I ran to join them. "Hey Mfuwetu, wait for me!" I ran after them and caught up when they got to the Ford truck, the one with no wheels, the upside-down one . . .

MARION (*confused, dislocated*). . . . I was at the stove, heating gravy for the roast beef, drinking red wine . . .

---

18 A fart?

SOLOMON. . . . Then I saw that Douglass was holding a gun, a real one, and that Jonathan had his hands tied behind his back with plastic that you find oranges in. Jonathan was making drowning sounds—he was crying—I saw he pissed in his pants and so I also started to cry.

MARION. . . . Anne was feeding Michael in his high chair and he was laughing and spitting out his food. The phone rang, Frank answered . . . and then it was like he was holding his breath, like he ran out of air, like green wobbly jelly, and there was a nudge in my being that I didn't want to answer . . . but Anne was laughing and . . .

SOLOMON. . . . Douglass screamed at me! "*Vok* off you devil, if you tell anyone I will kill you and all of your family! *Vok* off! *Voetsak!*"[19]

As I turned to go, Jonathan said something to me. It was a message for you. That is why I am here. That is why I have been coming here, to give you the message.

Silence. Making direct contact for the first time.

MARION. That was seven years ago.

SOLOMON. Yes.

MARION. And you have only come now.

SOLOMON. Yes.

MARION. What did he say? My boy. (*She grabs Solomon and shakes him*) What did he say?

SOLOMON. He said "Solomon, please tell my mother, I wasn't scared."

She lets out a small cry.

MARION. He said that?

SOLOMON. Yes.

MARION. But he was scared? (*Cries.*)

SOLOMON. Yes.

MARION. He was crying? He was crying, tell me more, more, tell me everything . . . (*She pours herself some more wine, and tries to keep back the tears.*)

SOLOMON. And then I turned and ran. (*Pause*) And then I heard the shot.

---

19 "Fuck . . . ! Fuck off! Get lost!"

MARION. The shot. Oh Christ! Oh God! Oh Christ! (*Crumples.*)

SOLOMON. When the boys were arrested I was too scared to say anything, everyone knew how dangerous they were.

MARION. They got off, you know that? A technicality, a botch-up by the police.

SOLOMON. Yes, I know.

MARION. You could have helped. If you had owned up, they would have been put away.

SOLOMON. I know. But they had many friends. If I had said something, they would have sent their friends to kill me. Hang me or burn me or rape my sister or even my grandmother. They are like dogs that take the meat from the table. They feel nothing. And, anyway, one year later, Douglass was shot by the police during a robbery at a supermarket. So he got his punishment.

MARION. I read about that.

So why did you come now? What makes you so brave now? I could tell the police that the other two are still alive.

SOLOMON. Would you do that? I will tell them if you want me to. The other two are anyway still making trouble in the township. I am still scared of them. I am still scared that they might hurt me or my sister.

MARION. Please! And open all that up again. The newspapers, the television. The photos of my boy on the front page. Lying naked in the scrapyard. The speculation: was he gay? Was he involved in drugs? Anything to make it not arbitrary. Anything to substantiate why he was asking for it. Why it could happen to him but not to someone else. Are they all fucking blind? This country has been breeding murderers for the past century. Isn't that clear. There doesn't need to be a reason. Anger, despair! That's the reason! That's the motivation. Isn't it obvious? But why my boy? Why mine? Why not somebody else's?

Then they come with—"Well, there has been violence in poor communities for decades now"—I know that! We know that. But does that make it any better? What? If we can't distribute the wealth, then at least we have succeeded in the equal distribution of violence. Does that make sense? Is there any sense in that? I don't know, perhaps there is. Perhaps there is. (*Silence.*)

"UCT Law Student Shot Dead." "Young Man Hijacked and Found Dead in a Scrapyard."

You know it was a new car? We had just bought it for him, again at my insistence . . . "Mother of Murdered Boy Collapses at His Funeral." On and on and on and on.

The pain never goes away, Solomon, but it's mine, no one else's, I need it to be mine.

That's why me and Frank lost each other at that time. He would sit staring at a chessboard—It was the one thing that he and Jonathan did together—play chess. And then I would walk into the lounge and see him with tears rolling down his face, and all it did was make me angry. Do you know, he let them give me shock therapy? He signed the documents. Marion Banning having shock therapy. It takes your pain away, you know? It sort of lies beside you like a book on a coffee table. For a while, anyway, it's not inside of you. But not for long, it comes back . . . and then you learn to keep it a secret . . . I could have reached out I suppose, to Frank—and he could have to me. That was the problem—we didn't know how to reach one another. A lifetime together and no way of reaching.

SOLOMON. When I got sick with the liver, when I was in hospital . . . I started to have dreams. The same dream. Jonathan saying, "Solomon, tell my mother I wasn't scared." Then Jonathan's face becomes my face, and then the shot wakes me up.

In my culture, the last person to see someone alive is supposed to speak at the funeral. You are supposed to tell the listeners what you saw and what you heard so that the living can be at peace with the whole story, with the truth around the death. I've been coming here for years, watching you—trying to find the right time. Carrying this thing with me. Walking with it.

If you do not do this, then you can become sick, you can be cursed with bad memories and bad dreams. I think that is why I got so sick.

Then last year I went to the mountain, I became a man. On the mountain we are taught to face our responsibilities.

MARION. So now your task is fulfilled?

SOLOMON. Yes. I'm so sorry, Mies Marion. I did not want to make your heart sore again.

MARION. So, now your job is done? No more bad dreams?

SOLOMON. I think it will be fine now.

MARION. So, you are a man? You can go! Mission accomplished.

SOLOMON. Yes, Mies Marion. I have delivered the message.

MARION. Good. Then off you go, Solomon. (*He stands*) Take the rest of the stew. (*He looks around for a packet*) Take the pot. (*He does so.*)

SOLOMON. Goodbye, Mies Marion.

MARION. Goodbye, Solomon. (*He shuts the door.*) Jonathan. Jonathan. Jonathan.

(*Music. Transition. Lights fade up on Marion at her desk.*)

And then he left, and hasn't been back in over two weeks.

You understand, Anne? That is why he has been visiting me. To deliver our Jonathan's message.

I don't know if you remember that time when Jonathan went on a school outing to the Science Museum. He was in Grade Two, all of seven years old. They were supposed to be dropped off at the school at one, and I was to pick Johno up at two-thirty. He was staying on for cricket. When I got to the school, he wasn't there. I asked some of his friends if they had seen him and they said he hadn't been at cricket practice. I immediately panicked and phoned his teacher. She said that she had last seen him at the Museum and she thinks that he was returned to the classroom at one. "You *think* he was returned!?" I screamed. "Are you fucking mad? What do you mean you 'think?'" I slammed down the phone, jumped into my car and sped off to the Museum. I cried all the way there and prayed to God that he was all right. When I got there, he was sitting on the floor next to the skeleton of a great white shark and sobbing to himself. He was terrified that he would have to stay there the whole night. The stupid bitch at the front desk had said that he was not allowed to use the phone and that he should use the call box. He had lost his card and was too embarrassed to ask for money. The next day when I took him to school, I grabbed his teacher, Mrs. Gibbs, by her stringy hair and said, "Don't you ever do that to my child again, you stupid, idiotic, excuse for a teacher."

Then she started to cry, and Jonathan started to cry, and it was pandemonium. I took Jonathan outside to console him and he said, "Mom, why are you still so angry? I have almost forgotten about it." And I said, "Jonathan my boy, I just never ever, ever want you to be scared."

Do you think that's what the message is about, Anne? I can't think that it can be anything else.

Do you think perhaps he remembered that day? Why that message? Why—"Tell my mother I wasn't scared." (*Pause.*)

Anne, dear, I wish we could put our differences aside now. That huge fight we had the last time we saw each other, honestly, it still haunts me. You saying that I had chosen to stay with a dead son rather than leave with a healthy daughter and two grandsons.

It's not that I am angry at you for saying it. It's that I am angry at myself for having made you feel so wretched. I do love you, my darling . . .

It's not that I don't want to be with you. It's just that I can't leave my home, please try to understand this, my girl.

Oh Anne, I'm not sure that I can continue.

Lights fade. Music. Transition. Marion is sitting on the couch. She is almost catatonic. Far away, lost. It is morning. The door opens. Pause. Solomon walks in carrying a box.

SOLOMON. Good morning, Mies Marion. (*Silence. He looks at her. She is very still.*) Mies Marion? Are you okay?

MARION (*Like coming out of a coma, confused, weak*). Solomon?

SOLOMON. Yes, Mies Marion. Are you okay? Look, I brought us a television. Mies Marion, how long have you been sitting here? Are you okay? Look, Mies Marion, I've bought us a television.

MARION (*nods*). Oh.

SOLOMON. Let me unpack it. (*Putting the box down.*)

MARION. Solomon, my boy, would you help me up? I need to go to the bathroom. I think I might have had a small accident. The old legs are tired.

SOLOMON. Yes, Mies Marion.

He helps her up, and takes her to the bathroom. He looks at the cushion where she has been sitting. He checks to see that she is still in the bathroom, then he turns the cushion round and puts a blanket over it. He begins to unpack the TV. Marion returns in a fresh nightgown and sits down on the couch.

MARION. That's better. (*Pause*) I haven't seen you for a while, Solomon.

SOLOMON. Yes, Mies Marion. I got a job picking pineapples, just temporary. So I'll have time to come and see you again.

MARION. Good, that will be nice. So you got us a TV?

SOLOMON. Yes. Color!

MARION. Is it already the World Cup?

SOLOMON. No, Mies Marion. But I thought we could just get it ready in the meantime.

MARION. Right. A stitch in time . . . Solomon, there is a letter on my desk. Would you mind posting it for me.

SOLOMON. No problem.

MARION. I've been thinking about going to see my daughter for a week or two.

SOLOMON. As long as you don't die there.

MARION. No. No. This is my home. I die here!

SOLOMON (*picking up the television*). Should I put it here on this table?

He places it in front of the couch. She reaches out to him to sit down. They look at the silent box.

MARION. Looks good.

SOLOMON. I'll have to get an extension cord.

MARION. Yes. Maybe you can borrow one.

SOLOMON. Yes, Mies Marion, I'll borrow one.

MARION. Solomon, my boy, do you have to continually use that old subservient term "Mies Marion?" It's what your grandmother called me.

SOLOMON. Mies is not always a subservient term, Mies Marion. Mies can also be a term of . . . Of care. Of caring.

MARION. What, Solomon? Are you saying you care about me?

SOLOMON. I'm not sure what I'm saying, Mies Marion.

MARION. Solomon?

SOLOMON. Yes, Mies Marion?

MARION. Thank you!

Lights fade to black.

End of Play

FROM LEFT TO RIGHT: *Brian Webber (Boss)* and *Tsepo Wa Mamatu (Vusi). Photograph by Sally Gaule.*

ARMED RESPONSE

DAVID PEIMER

FROM LEFT TO RIGHT: *Lunga Radebe* (*Themba*) *and Tsepo Wa Mamatu* (*Vusi*). *Photograph by Sally Gaule*.

VUSI	employee of Armed Response, in his early 30s
ANNA	23, from Germany
ZAMA	Vusi's friend, in his late 20s
THEMBA	gangster, in his late 20s
LERATO	26, TV actress, Anna's neighbor
BRENDA	28, housewife, Anna's neighbor
INSPECTOR	early 40s
BOSS	late 30s
PRIVATE SECURITY GUARD	voice offstage
2 POLICEWOMEN	voices on the phone

SET: Johannesburg. Anna's living room is on a raised platform, upstage right. Sofa, chairs, low coffee table. There is a fridge on the platform, against the back wall. The entrance to her living room is offstage right. At specific times during the play, burglar bars are put up. Eventually they surround her living room, creating a large cage.

A bar counter and stools are upstage left, raised.

This area doubles as a police station with a desk and two chairs.

The street outside Anna's house is the whole downstage area. A pile of bricks is on the floor, downstage left.

Armed Response was first performed at Johannesburg, 2006.

VUSI	Tsepho Wa Mamatu
ANNA	Tarryn Lee
ZAMA	Jerry Mntonga
THEMBA	Lunga Radebe
LERATO	Lali Dangazele
BRENDA	Martina Griller
INSPECTOR	Lebo Motaung
BOSS	Brian Webber
MUGGER	Raymond Ngomane
DIRECTOR	David Peimer

Scene 1

There is a large screen in front of the audience which conceals the stage. The advert is projected on the screen.

VOICEOVER (*announces in the dark*). Ladies and gentlemen, this is your Captain speaking. Welcome aboard African Airlines, Flight 701 from Berlin to Johannesburg.

The advert and the voiceover below are simultaneous.

Opening shot: *MGM Lion roaring, then beautiful picture of Table Mountain, then brief safari images. Alluring images of high walls, barbed wire, electric fences, men with machine guns in military gear guarding homes and buildings (filmed from below like war heroes); call center with highly sophisticated electronic equipment, hundreds of employees with headsets on phones, lights flashing, screens of maps. A car from the company Armed Response arrives at a house. Armed men jump out and rush in.*

We see a smiling woman with her child.

During the advert, we hear light jazzy music and the following voiceover:

VOICEOVER. South Africa, where the sun always shines.

When you arrive, contact the Armed Response Security Company.

We have thousands of cars patrolling the streets at all times. Our highly trained team will be at your home within seconds to keep you safe, and alive. We care about you, your family, your property. We build fortress-high walls, alarms, electrified fences.

Trust Armed Response for your Private Security. We keep you safe. (*Pause*) Have a restful flight.

Close-up of lion purring, licking its paws. Image fades. Screen is lifted.

Scene 2

Anna's house. She has just arrived from Germany the day before, some suitcases are still unpacked. Anna wears jeans and a shirt with the sleeves rolled up. She is barefoot. Standing on a chair, she is busy putting up a poster. The doorbell rings.

ANNA. Come in. (*The doorbell rings again.*) It's open!

Vusi enters. He wears a suit and tie, and carries a stylish briefcase.

VUSI. Hello?

ANNA. Morning! You must be my neighbor. Get you coffee in a minute.

VUSI. You forgot to lock your front door.

ANNA. I like it open. Can you help me with this, please?

Vusi puts down his briefcase and helps her with the poster.

VUSI. You really should lock it.

ANNA. No. Makes me feel like I'm in a prison.

VUSI. It's dangerous. (*Pause*) I'm not a neighbor. I work for Armed Response Security Company.

ANNA. Nice to meet you. I'm Anna. I saw your ad on the plane.

VUSI. You just arrived?

ANNA. Yes, left Germany a few days ago. Minus 20 there. And here I am—in the middle of summer.

VUSI. So you're a German . . .

ANNA. Yes.

VUSI. You don't have an accent.

ANNA. My Mum's English.

VUSI. I see . . . What are you doing in South Africa?

ANNA. I'm a photographer. Came here to take pictures. Always wanted to come here. Germany is so . . . regulated.

VUSI. . . . a photographer. . . .

ANNA. Doing a series for a magazine. On the music scene here. My first.

VUSI. I see . . . So, where you going to get your photos?

ANNA. Usual places. Bars, clubs, also meet the bands. But what I really want is to get the night scene in Soweto. Read about those places. What do you call them . . . *shebeen*s. Are they really all run by mothers?

VUSI. You want to go to Soweto . . . at night?

ANNA. Listen, I'm not here for the Big Five. I love cities. Cities with an edge . . .

Vusi sits down. They have finished putting up the poster.

VUSI. I don't think that's a good idea.

ANNA. You're sweet. But I'll be fine. I know how to handle myself. Besides, I never had a problem before.

VUSI. You haven't been here before.

ANNA. I've been around. Saw your ad on the plane.

VUSI. Oh . . . good. I've brought you the contract.

ANNA. What contract?

VUSI. Your private security contract with Armed Response.

ANNA (*laughs*). That's very kind of you, but I don't need it.

VUSI. Every house in this street is with us. Attacks occur quite frequently in this area, you know.

ANNA. Well, I've got nothing worth stealing. Just my camera, and I always take it with me.

VUSI. I'm not talking about your camera.

ANNA. Look, I know about the crime here. But I'm not paying any company to do what the police do.

VUSI (*smiles*). And what would that be?

ANNA. The usual. (*Laughing*) In Germany, they're so organized, they arrest you if you throw a plastic bottle in the green rubbish bin.

VUSI. Green . . . bin?

ANNA. Yes, green is for glass bottles, blue is for metal and yellow for plastic.

VUSI. You can't be serious.

ANNA. I am. There're three rubbish bins on every street corner. Just for bottles!

VUSI. Here, the bins would disappear in a minute! (*They laugh. He looks at some of her pictures on the table.*) Did you take these?

ANNA. No, that's my family.

VUSI (*flipping through the pictures*). This is you! . . . How old?

ANNA. Thirteen. That explains the haircut.

They both smile.

VUSI. Is this your father?

ANNA (*curtly*). Yes. Here, these are some of mine.

VUSI (*looking at them*). Did you take this one with a red filter?

ANNA. Yes. How did you know?

Silence.

VUSI. My . . . sister was a photographer.

ANNA. Was?

VUSI. She . . . got shot.

Pause.

ANNA. What happened?

VUSI. A riot. Years ago. She was taking pictures.

ANNA. I'm sorry.

VUSI. It's okay.

ANNA (*pause, gently*). What was her name?

VUSI. Zenande.

ANNA. She must have been brave. (*Pause. Holds out the contract.*) Really, I don't need it.

Vusi puts it on the table.

VUSI. . . . I'm sure you'll reconsider. (*Goes to the door, turns, smiles warmly at Anna*) Welcome to Johannesburg. (*Leaves.*)

Scene 3

The bar. Cans of beer. Zama is waiting for Vusi. Vusi enters. Zama gives him a beer.

VUSI. Hey, Zama. How's things?

ZAMA. They bullied my kid!

VUSI. Who?

ZAMA. Kids at his school. Fucking hell! You should have seen him. Spent the whole night polishing his shoes, ironing his new white Woolworth's shirt.

VUSI. Not the PEP Stores one?

ZAMA. PEP Stores? My kid will never look like the son of a postmaster from Benoni!

VUSI. Okay, so he had the Woolworth's shirt on. What happened?

ZAMA. It's his first day. I do his tie. Off he goes. Full uniform. With his little lunch box. Cheese sandwiches. Cheddar.

VUSI. Neatly sliced.

ZAMA. How do you know?

VUSI. You always slice your sandwiches neatly. Two pieces of bread, cut into four.

ZAMA. Well, he gets there. These three boys grab him. Big boys. Really big. They were never that big in our day. They take him to a *donga*.[1] Fuck him up so bad he can hardly walk. Tomorrow, those kids and their fathers are going to know who Zama is! (*Shouting*) Zola! Bring me another Lion! Where the hell is Zola? Tomorrow, that school is going to hear from me!

VUSI. Good. This new generation. Bullying little kids. Full of shit.

ZAMA (*pause*). So, you got the last contract in the street. Tonight, we celebrate!

VUSI. No party tonight.

ZAMA. Huh?

VUSI (*exasperated*). She didn't take it!

ZAMA. What?! Why not? What happened?

VUSI. We . . . talked.

ZAMA. You talked?

VUSI. No big deal. About . . . her job, me, family stuff . . .

ZAMA. All that shit? To a client? I know that look of yours. You dig her, man!

VUSI. She's just a kid.

ZAMA. Where have I heard that before. Just say it. You like the girl.

VUSI. I want her to sign the contract. That's all!

ZAMA. Okay, okay, when do you want me and Themba to go twist her sweet little arm?

VUSI. She's going to take pictures in Soweto—at night. She'll learn.

ZAMA. No shortage of teachers there!

Pause.

VUSI (*reflecting*). I hope she'll be okay. She doesn't even lock her front door.

---

1 . . . ditch.

ZAMA. What is it about this girl?

VUSI. She listens to music, takes photos, talks . . .

ZAMA. What girl on the planet doesn't listen to music, take photos, talk?

VUSI. She's . . . not scared. Says what's on her mind.

ZAMA. Ever met a girl who doesn't? That's why they drive us to drink!

Themba walks into the bar.

THEMBA. Hey man, how's the kid?

ZAMA. He'll be okay. Tomorrow, me and my wife are going to speak to the principal.

THEMBA. Good. (*To Vusi*) Did you get the contract?

VUSI. No problem. Have it done in a few days.

THEMBA. So you didn't get it.

ZAMA. Themba, tell us about your new girl from Senegal. Vusi, she's stunning.

VUSI. Themba, there are two kinds of people. Those who lift you. And those who drain you. You drain me. (*Vusi's cellphone rings*) . . . Boss! Everything's fine . . . *Ja* . . . Thursday . . . She's got it. (*Joking*) You know—she's German, they want to look at all the small print first. . . . Sure I'll get it! Be the biggest contract in the whole street . . . that's why it'll take a few more days. . . . Thanks, Boss. (*He switches the phone off.*)

Pause.

THEMBA. How's the boss?

VUSI. Fine. Zola! Where is he? I want a beer. Zola! If you want anything done in this country, you have to do it yourself. (*Exits to get a beer.*)

THEMBA. Zama, aren't you tired?

ZAMA. Huh?

THEMBA. Tired of doing the dirty work? For him? You know he only got the fancy job because his cousin knows the Boss. He's connected. We're the cleaners. I've had enough of the nightshift. I should be selling. I'd sell thousands, fast—no bullshit waiting for some bitch to read the small print!

ZAMA. Not again! I've heard this shit a thousand times before.

THEMBA. Well, who does he think he is? You remember that day? Outside our school. Thousands of cops. The four of us . . . Zenande taking pictures. We threw the stones. Hit one of them on the head. So they start shooting. Everything goes mad. She gets shot. And what does Vusi do? Runs away. To read his fucking books. Leaves his sister. A coward, that's what he is. (*Pause*) Who had time for books in those days? Now he's the one with a fancy car, big house . . . I deserve more, much more.

ZAMA. Nobody gets what they deserve. (*Pause*) Wake up, man! It's another century. We're businessmen now. I got a family now. Kids. A kid who goes to a school of bullies!

Vusi enters, drinking.

VUSI. Zola's got more piss in him than an elephant! When's he going to learn how to run a business?! Come on Themba, take us to meet your beauty.

Exit.

Scene 4

Anna's house. Her neighbors, Brenda and Lerato are visiting. There is a cake on the table. They are drinking champagne.

BRENDA. Welcome to our street, Anna!

LERATO. It's cool to have a real European as my next-door neighbor.

BRENDA. And one who invites us for cake!

LERATO. This never happens in Greenside.

BRENDA. Or anywhere in Jo'burg.

LERATO. So you're German?

ANNA. Uhuh.

BRENDA. My brother just got back from traveling through Europe. Hitched everywhere. Said the Germans were really friendly. Germans and Greeks.

LERATO. I had this Greek boyfriend last year. Friendly isn't the word. He was fire!

ANNA. Where is he now?

LERATO. Back in fuck-knows-where-polis.

They laugh. They keep drinking throughout the scene.

ANNA (*to Lerato*). Another piece?

LERATO. No, thanks. Have to watch my figure for the shooting.

ANNA. Shooting?

BRENDA. Lerato is a famous TV actress. On "*Isithando*."[2] Most popular soap in the country.

ANNA. Sorry, never heard of it.

LERATO. You haven't?

ANNA. No. More champagne?

LERATO. Yes, thanks.

Brenda has discovered Anna's pictures of Hillbrow on the coffee table.

BRENDA. Is this . . . Hillbrow? Tiny baby in a shoebox . . .

ANNA. Yes, I took those yesterday.

LERATO. A shoebox? Let's see. That place is full of slimy Nigerians, filthy Zimbabweans . . .

BRENDA. Who did you go with?

ANNA. Went on my own.

BRENDA. What?!

LERATO. You can't be serious?

BRENDA. You were lucky. Just don't ever do that again, please.

LERATO. You can't just go to those places.

BRENDA. Anywhere, you have to be so careful. Just the other day, my friend stopped at a stop street.[3] Some guy smashes the window, tries to grab her cellphone. She holds onto it. So he bites her hand. Can you believe it? Bites her hand!

LERATO. There's so much of it happening. Everywhere. (*Pause. They drink more. To Anna*) I'm a very cautious person. Last week—I'm driving home. When I check my rear-view mirror, someone is following me. I'm sure of it. So I'm thinking fast. Don't go into the driveway, drive past—get onto the highway, only get off at Midrand and head straight for the mall. I get to the mall.

---

2 "The Loved One"—a satirical name for one of the most popular soap operas in South Africa called "Isidingo" ("The Need").

3 "Stop street" here is an abbreviation for a stop sign in the street.

There's been some big robbery. Bank or something. Everyone's going crazy. But I go to my hairdresser. Luigi. He's Greek . . . I think. Or maybe Italian. Anyway, you'll get to meet him. Everyone goes to Luigi. He's the best. Knows all the latest styles. Don't worry, he does ordinary people, not only celebrities.

BRENDA. This woman I work with. Her sister was hijacked just last month. They locked her in the boot. Drove around forever. She thought it was the end. After a few hours they dumped her at the side of the road.

LERATO. Luigi's boyfriend was shot dead in broad daylight. Center of town. For his cellphone and his watch.

BRENDA. My gardener had his head smashed in with a hammer. In his bed, at night. He's still in a coma.

Pause. They drink.

ANNA. Why are you telling me all this?

BRENDA. You shouldn't be going to Hillbrow.

LERATO. Or out at night on your own.

BRENDA. Don't walk anywhere. Drive.

LERATO. Car doors locked, panic button on your key.

BRENDA. Get an electric fence for your house.

LERATO. Make the walls very high.

BRENDA. With sharp spikes on top.

LERATO. Put panic buttons in every room.

BRENDA. Make sure they're linked to a private security company.

LERATO. Keep a gun next to your bed!

ANNA. . . . sounds like a state of war . . .

Silence. They drink more champagne.

BRENDA. Never thought of it like that. There's so much violence everywhere.

LERATO. It's just a case of knowing the dos and don'ts.

BRENDA. You get used to it.

LERATO. Read about fencing off the whole city.

BRENDA. The whole city?

LERATO. Every inch.

BRENDA. But where do we put the criminals?

BRENDA AND LERATO. Nigeria! (*They both laugh.*)

BRENDA. Luigi really is good. You look wonderful.

LERATO. Wanted these streaks for ages.

BRENDA. Maybe I should go to him.

LERATO. He's the best. You know, he went to a gypsy festival in Bohemia over Christmas.

BRENDA. Really? Bohemia?

LERATO. Goes every year.

BRENDA. But I feel committed to Enzo. You know I've been with him for years.

LERATO. That, my friend, is a problem. A very big problem.

BRENDA. Enzo is really good, got a feel for hair. And he looks like Johnny Depp.

LERATO. He does?

BRENDA. I swear.

They both chuckle and drink some more champagne.

ANNA. This is crazy.

BRENDA. Enzo?

LERATO. Luigi?

ANNA. No, the stuff you were talking about before.

BRENDA. Anna, you must join Armed Response.

LERATO. Everyone in our street is with AR.

ANNA. I'm not.

LERATO. What?

BRENDA. Why not?

ANNA. I don't want to.

BRENDA. But you need it!

ANNA. Why should I have to pay for something like that?

BRENDA. Haven't you heard a word of what we've been saying?

ANNA. I heard you.

BRENDA. Then why risk your life?

LERATO. This is not Europe.

ANNA. I know that.

LERATO. I don't think you do!

BRENDA. My husband's a doctor. You know what he sees every day?

ANNA. I can imagine.

BRENDA. I don't think you can.

LERATO. We're trying to be helpful.

ANNA. Please, don't patronize me.

BRENDA. You must take out a contract.

LERATO. You also have to think of us.

ANNA. What do you mean?

BRENDA (*pause*). If there's one unprotected house in the area, the gangs get to know about it.

LERATO. And that attracts them.

BRENDA. They swarm into the whole area.

LERATO. Like thousands of hungry mosquitoes.

BRENDA. Itching for our blood.

LERATO (*pause*). We're worried about you.

ANNA. Thank you. I think I know how to take care of myself.

Pause.

LERATO. Brenda, it's getting late.

BRENDA. You're right. We should go. Self-defence class starts in five minutes.

They start to leave.

ANNA. Thank you for the visit.

Brenda and Lerato exit.

Scene 5

Anna's house. She is organizing her things. Doorbell rings.

ANNA. It's open!

Vusi enters whistling "Dead Dog Blues".

VUSI. Hi, how've you been?

ANNA. Fine. Want a beer?

VUSI. Er . . . no thanks. Have you thought about the contract?

ANNA. Yes, it's on the table.

VUSI. Still not locking your door?

ANNA. No. Sure you don't want one?

VUSI. . . . Okay. (*Pause, she gets him a beer. He sits down and looks at the photographs*) Been to all these places?

ANNA. A few. Hillbrow is something. Seething with people. From everywhere. Desperate people.

VUSI (*pause*). I hope nothing happened to you?

ANNA. I was fine. There was something going on in a street. But it was further down.

VUSI. This continent. Either it puts you in a killing rage or merely tosses you in front of a stray bullet.

ANNA. Poetic. Nice. (*She motions to her pictures.*)

VUSI. You've taken a lot. These are very good.

ANNA. Thanks. It's . . . like a way of stopping time.

VUSI. How do you mean?

ANNA. It sounds silly.

VUSI. No, please tell me.

ANNA (*pause*). When I was a child, I used to take my camera. Look at something. Ordinary things. A sunset, a face, my dog. Look at it. I mean really look at it. I knew it wouldn't last . . .

VUSI. But you wanted to hold on to it.

ANNA. Exactly!

Pause.

VUSI. You really love your work. (*Silence. He searches amongst papers and pictures on the table. He finds the contract.*) Looks like you've spilled some coffee on it.

ANNA (*laughing*). Sorry.

VUSI. You forgot to sign.

ANNA. Told you. I don't see why I should have to pay for what the police are supposed to do.

Pause.

VUSI. Anna, you live in Johannesburg now. Big shit can happen to you.

ANNA. You're being quite pushy. I told you I don't see why I should have to.

VUSI. For Christ's sake! I'm trying to help you, woman!

ANNA (*shocked*). Excuse me? Who do you think you're shouting at?

VUSI. I'm sorry . . . Please . . . Please . . . Just listen . . . In the last month two houses in this street were hit. People got tied up, kicked in the face. One is still in hospital.

Pause.

ANNA. Two houses in the last month? So what's the point of a contract anyway?

Silence.

VUSI. Look, I . . . don't want anything to happen to you.

ANNA. What are you saying?

VUSI. I'm saying you're in danger.

ANNA. From who?

VUSI. Guys who will rape or kill for a few bucks! (*Pause*) You want to go back to Europe in a coffin?

ANNA. Listen, I've been going out. For a week now. And nothing's happened. I'm fine.

VUSI. You are so stubborn! You know the city breathes violence. Thinks violence. Every minute. Every day.

ANNA. What's your point?

VUSI. In Hillbrow, did you see a cop?

ANNA. No

VUSI. Soweto? Also, no cops. And why? Because either they get kickbacks or couldn't give a shit. That's why you need private protection.

ANNA. Why are you so pushy about this? Anyone else would just accept what I want and leave it. But you don't stop. You push and push. You're just like the Mafia. You sell fear. So people pay you.

VUSI. We're not a Mafia!

Silence. Anna takes a step back, looks at Vusi.

ANNA (*coldly*). You seemed really nice the first time we met. (*Pause*) I'm going for a walk. You'll be gone when I get back.

VUSI. Walk . . . now . . . in the dark?!

ANNA. Yes.

VUSI. Anna! Wait!

ANNA. Switch off the lights when you leave.

She exits. Pause. Zama and Themba come in.

ZAMA. What happened?

THEMBA. What did you do to her, Vusi?

ZAMA. She was seriously pissed off, man.

VUSI. What you doing here?

ZAMA. Came to help.

THEMBA. Back-up. In case you fuck up.

VUSI. We'll talk about this later. She'll get attacked out there. I have to check it out.

ZAMA. Why you so worried about her?

VUSI. I haven't got time for this Zama. You wait here, I'll follow her to make sure she gets home safe.

ZAMA. What?!

THEMBA. I know what he's thinking. If something happens in the street, it's not in the house. Streets don't have contracts. So when she gets back, we give her a Number 3 in her house.

VUSI. Number 1 will be enough.

THEMBA. Number 2.

VUSI. One!

Vusi runs out after Anna. Themba and Zama wait in her house.

Scene 6

Anna's house. Themba and Zama are waiting for her in the dark. It's pitch black. Themba is terrified of the dark. He whispers. Zama speaks normally.

THEMBA. Zama?

ZAMA. *Ja.*

THEMBA. Really dark in here.

ZAMA. *Ja.*

THEMBA. What you doing, man? (*Silence*) Zama!

ZAMA. What?

THEMBA. I can't see you!

ZAMA. So?

THEMBA. Where are you?

ZAMA. Lying down.

THEMBA. Why?

ZAMA. Shut up, I'm tired.

> *Silence.*

THEMBA. Zama? (*Silence*) Zama!!? (*We hear Zama snoring*) Shit! Zama wake up! Don't do this to me! Wake up! What the fuck . . . where's the . . . why couldn't Vusi leave the lights on? I can't see anything!

> *Themba goes to the fridge and opens the door. The only light on stage comes out of the fridge.*

ZAMA (*half-asleep, annoyed*). What you doing, man?

THEMBA. Nothing, just . . . it's so dark in here.

ZAMA. Does she have any beer?

THEMBA. No. . . . *Eish!* This cheese is off! All moldy and blue! (*Reading the label*) Gor . . . gon . . . zo . . . la.

ZAMA. It's blue cheese, man.

THEMBA. No shit! Where does this stuff come from?

ZAMA. It's Italian.

THEMBA. Europeans! They're all white but their cheese is blue!

ZAMA. You're a darkie who's scared of the dark.

THEMBA. I am not!

ZAMA. Close the fridge then!

Pause.

THEMBA. No . . . I'm busy here.

ZAMA. Busy keeping the light on while I'm trying to sleep.

THEMBA. I'm hungry, man.

ZAMA (*sees Anna's pictures on the table*). What's this? (*Uses his lighter to look more closely. Themba eats the cheese with cucumber*) Man! This is my old school in Soweto! Had a serious paint job. Pink walls—who paints a school in a *moffie*[4] color? I'll have to speak to Mr. Radebe about this. In my day we would have burnt the school down if it was pink!

THEMBA. Ours was gray. Still burnt it down.

ZAMA. No wonder you know nothing about Italian cheese.

THEMBA (*with his mouth full*). Gor-gon-zo-la. Tastes good with cucumber. School of life. Who needs teachers?

ZAMA (*looking at another picture*). This is the street! Where they bullied my kid.

THEMBA. Little gangsters! Kids of today. They know nothing. If I was president, I'd have all the bullies shot!

They eat more cheese as the lights fade.

Scene 7

The street that night. Anna walks across the stage. She exits. A woman, wearing a track suit with a hood covering her head, comes on jogging. Vusi rushes after her holding a gun. He grabs her from behind, holds the gun to her head.

VUSI. Don't move! (*Pause*) Get lost or I'll make you eat your fucking balls.

WOMAN. Please don't hurt me! Here—my watch, my money. Take it . . . my phone . . . (*She holds it out.*)

VUSI. What?

WOMAN. . . . Don't kill me!

---

4 South African slang meaning "effeminate."

VUSI (*pulls her hood off*). You're a woman? (*Pause*) What you doing here?

WOMAN. . . . . Jogging.

VUSI. You should be at home!

WOMAN. It's . . . just round the block.

VUSI. You hurry back . . . you hear me? (*Woman runs off, leaving her stuff on the ground.*) Hey, lady! Wait! You forgot your things! (*She comes back, picks them up, and leaves, terrified.*) And lock your door!

Anna enters, walking in deep thought. She sits on the pile of bricks. Mugger with knife enters from the opposite side of the street. He stands, looking at her, then quietly moves up behind her. Vusi enters silently behind the mugger. He puts his hand over the man's mouth and holds a gun to his head. In silence, Vusi pulls the mugger offstage. Anna is unaware of what's happening. We hear a gun shot offstage. Anna is startled. She gets up and walks off quickly back to her house.

Scene 8

Vusi enters near the pile of bricks. He looks at Anna's house to make sure she's safely inside. Anna switches the lights on. Her house is brightly lit. Vusi withdraws offstage. Themba and Zama leap to their feet.

ANNA (*frightened*). Who are you? . . . What do you want?

Instantly, Themba grabs Anna. He stands behind her, forcibly ties a rope around her throat.

THEMBA. Nice to meet you, sweetheart. (*Zama walks slowly to the light switch and turns it off. He stands and watches. Themba holds the rope around her neck with his one hand and lights his lighter with the other. He moves it across her face. Anna panics and starts kicking and fighting. She kicks Themba hard on the shin. He stifles a shout*) Bitch! (*Themba lets Anna go, she turns around and knees him in the balls. He shouts in pain*) Aaaaaaah!

ZAMA. Let's go! (*Exits.*)

THEMBA (*hissing to Anna*). I'll get you for this!

Themba leaves. Anna switches the light on. She breathes heavily, rubbing her throat. Terrified, she looks around the house, notices that her photos have been scattered over the table. She goes to the fridge to get some water, notices the half-eaten cheese. She takes it out, looks at it and throws it away. She sits down anxiously, picks up the phone and dials. We hear a dialling tone, light music.

PRE-RECORDED VOICE. Welcome to Johannesburg Police . . . If you or your loved ones have been hijacked, please dial 1. If you or your loved ones have been shot, please dial 2. If you or your loved ones have been robbed, please dial 3. Otherwise hold for an operator . . . All our operators are currently busy. Your call is important to us. Please hold.

More light music.

ANNA. *Verdammte Scheisse!*[5] Pick up the phone, you bastards!

Light music.

VOICE 1. Thank you for calling Johannesburg Police Station. Thandi speaking—how can I help?

ANNA. I've just been attacked!

VOICE 1. I see . . . and where did this attack take place?

ANNA. In my house!

VOICE 1. Which area are you calling from?

ANNA. Greenside.

VOICE 1. Please hold while I put you through.

Light music comes back on.

ANNA. *Warten Sie! Das gibt's doch nicht! Scheisse!*[6]

VOICE 2. Thank you for calling Cape Town Police Station. Sepati speaking, how can I help you?

ANNA. Cape Town?!

VOICE 2. Yes. Which area are you calling from?

ANNA. I'm calling from Johannesburg, Greenside, they said they'd put me through to . . .

VOICE 2. Please hold.

Light music. Anna slams the phone down.

Scene 9

The bar, next evening. "Dead Dog Blues" song in the background. Vusi is drinking alone. He picks up his phone and calls Anna.

─────────────

5 Damn shit!
6 It can't be the truth!

VUSI. Hello Anna, it's Vusi . . . from Armed Response . . . I'm just calling to find out . . . What? . . . Are you okay? . . . I'll come now. . . . Why not . . . What are you saying? . . . Anna, I swear I had nothing to do with it. . . . I really think I should come . . . Anna, please let's talk . . . Anna! (*Anna has hung up. Vusi drinks his beer. Song continues underneath. His cellphone rings*) Hello? Boss . . . yes, I just spoke to her. . . . No, not yet. . . . she needs more time . . . Boss, just another two days, . . . I'm doing my best. A Number 5?! . . . No, wait, give me a chance. You'll have it by Monday. . . . yes, no one in the street can be without a contract . . . the neighbors know nothing . . . I won't let it spread.

Boss hangs up the phone. (*Song comes back up, softly*) *Vusi is sitting drinking. Silhouetted, on the platform, Anna is putting up the first set of bars over the window facing the street and along the back wall.*

Black out.

VUSI'S VOICE ON TAPE. That stupid kid. She doesn't believe in paying. She'll learn. Only one thing to believe in. War. Every day is war. We get a bit of time out. To be alone. Calm . . . they're just moments to load the artillery. For the next battle. (*Pause*) Used to love my books. Haven't read one for years. What did I do with them. What . . . did I . . . (*Pause*) Anna. What kind of name is that? Could kill her. Strangle the brat. Quick death. (*Pause*) Biology books. Wanted to find out how things worked. All gone now. All gone. (*Pause*) Got to keep the Boss happy. Sell my quota every month. (*Pause*) You were right, Zenande . . . I've always been scared to rock the boat. Been like that my whole life . . . (*Pause*) Like . . . sleeping with broken glass.

The song continues. Lights slowly fade.

Scene 10

The bar. Vusi drinking as before. Zama enters.

ZAMA. Hey, Vusi.

VUSI. How did it go with the principal?

ZAMA. Fucking arsehole!

VUSI. What happened?

ZAMA. He says he'll take care of it, but we must go "easy" on these kids. They're going through a "difficult phase." "Parents divorced, father lost his job, mother's got high blood pressure" . . . Can you believe this shit? Gives me high blood pressure!

VUSI. So what you're gonna do?

ZAMA. What can I do? If I cause too much shit, my kid will have it even harder. (*Pause*) Wife called me a loser.

Themba enters.

THEMBA. Look what your girl did to me! (*Shows Vusi his swollen balls*). Just when I was about to score with that native from up North!

ZAMA. Maybe you'll have to discuss Senegalese land reform policies instead.

THEMBA. Get fucked!

ZAMA. I will—my balls will see action tonight! So, Vusi, all sorted out now?

VUSI. No.

THEMBA. What? I get kicked in the balls for nothing! I'll kill her!

ZAMA. What happened? Thought we scared the shit out of her last night?!

VUSI. She thought she scared the shit out of you!

THEMBA. Us?

ZAMA. When I think about it, you did scream like a baby!

VUSI. She says she kicked you out herself. Doesn't need our help. No contract.

ZAMA. This kid's giving me a headache.

VUSI. She won't even see me. Boss is pissed off like hell. (*Pause*) Why does she have to be so German?

THEMBA. Told you we should have done a Number 3 on her. I need a drink first. Where's Zola? I want a beer. Zola! Probably pissed outside. I'll get it. (*Exits.*)

VUSI. What are you guys planning behind my back?

ZAMA. She's fucking with the business! This is not just about your contract—You know Vuyo? The one who puts in the alarms. (*Vusi nods*) He was fixing her neighbors' electric fence this morning.

VUSI. And?

ZAMA. They were going to upgrade big time this week. They're not any more. Your Anna's talked them out of it.

VUSI. What?!

ZAMA. She told them not to waste their money.

VUSI. . . . It's spreading . . .

ZAMA. Yes. Through the whole bloody area.

VUSI. . . . No need to panic . . . We give her neighbors a Number 3. That'll sort them out and shut her up.

ZAMA. We have to give it to the girl. She needs a lesson.

VUSI. . . . No . . .

ZAMA. Vusi, she's just a rich German kid. Come to take pictures of the natives.

VUSI. Leave her.

ZAMA (*pause*). Don't do this man. Don't lose everything you worked for.

VUSI. I said no. (*Pause.*) Zama, tell me why do people need us? I mean . . . police should be out there.

ZAMA. I don't believe I'm hearing this. You know what's out there. Remember your words . . . "a huge wave of killers . . . we're just the foam riding the wave . . . businessmen see opportunity where others see chaos." (*Pause*) You'll lose the whole street if you don't stop her.

Themba enters, drinking.

THEMBA. Let's go Zama! Maybe she's still got some of that cheese.

ZAMA. See you later, Vusi. You know this is right.

They exit, Vusi stays behind drinking. Pause. He calls Anna, listens to her voice mail message and leaves a message slightly altering his voice.

VUSI. Hello, this is Siswe Mopedi from the Johannesburg *Star* newspaper. We've heard about your work. I know this is a late notice but we're having an urgent meeting tonight at our offices downtown. We would like to discuss employing you part-time. Please meet me at seven and bring your portfolio.

Scene 11

The street that night. Themba, Zama arrive outside Anna's house.

THEMBA. Lights are off. She's out.

ZAMA. This window is barred. Let's go round the back.

Themba grabs a brick off the pile, they go offstage. We hear a window being smashed. Themba and Zama appear inside Anna's living room in the dark. They wait in silence.

Vusi appears outside the house. He puts on a balaclava, takes out a gun and waits in the dark street. Anna arrives carrying her portfolio. Vusi steps out of the shadows, grabs her, holds the gun to her head. She freezes. He blindfolds her.

ANNA. Please, what do you want? (*He pulls her downstage onto the street in front of the pile of bricks away from the house. He forces her down onto her knees, the piles of bricks blocking the view from the house.*) Listen, I'll give you anything you want. Please don't hurt me. (*Silence*) . . . Don't shoot. (*Silence. Vusi looks at the house to make sure Themba and Zama don't see him. He checks the time on his watch.*) My name's Anna . . . I'm just a photographer. . . . these are my pictures. . . . I had a phone call . . . just went to meet someone at his office . . . newspaper office . . . downtown . . . He called me, his name is Siswe. I waited an hour . . . But nobody came . . . Do you know him? (*Silence*) . . . Take my money, cellphone . . . everything. (*Silence. Anna reaches out and finds his hand. She holds it. Silence. She withdraws her hand*) . . . If you want sex, I'll do it . . . You don't have to rape me.

Vusi checks the house, Themba and Zama are still inside. Silence.

VUSI. Streets are dangerous

Silence.

ANNA (*vulnerable*). I thought . . .The nights are so warm. (*Pause*) I'm not from here. When I arrived, I couldn't wait to wake up to a hot sun every day. Vast blue skies . . . endless space. I loved the smell of the jacarandas. Especially at night. Walking outside . . . warm summer nights. Been here for a week . . . now all I want is to lock myself in. Bar up my windows. Don't trust anyone any more. (*Pause*) Where are you from? Do you have a girl? Family . . . sister?

Pause.

VUSI. Shut up . . . you talk too much . . . I should just finish it. Now. Had enough of you.

ANNA. . . . Please. . . .

Silence.

VUSI. Have you been on safari?

ANNA. . . . No.

VUSI. You need to see the animals. In the wild. Watch them carefully. Look at the little buck. Eyes wide open, ears twitching, alert, always scared, listening for danger. Learn from them.

Pause.

ANNA. Please . . . can I go?

Silence. Vusi looks at the house. Themba and Zama are leaving the house through the back window offstage—the way they came in.

VUSI. Learn to protect yourself. Put up an electric fence.

ANNA. . . . I will

VUSI. Burglar bars.

ANNA. . . . Yes.

VUSI. Get private security—Armed Response are good.

Anna nods. Silence.

He takes her blindfold off. He motions for her to go.

Anna goes into her house. Vusi leaves. Themba and Zama walk into the street.

ZAMA. Fuck this waiting shit. What do we do now?

THEMBA. What Vusi said—hit the neighbors.

They exit.

Scene 12

Police station. Anna and Brenda are waiting.

ANNA. Fucking blindfolded me! Talking crazy stuff. It was . . . How much longer do we have to wait?

BRENDA. It's only been two and a half hours.

ANNA. Only?!

BRENDA. Anna, I'm as upset as you. My husband had both his legs broken. And I have to sit in this police station all day while he needs me in the hospital.

Pause.

ANNA. I'm sorry.

Silence.

BRENDA. Police are useless. Called them four times last night . . . kept getting that stupid music. And their answering machine. Left four messages! Did they bother to call back?

ANNA. Great way of dealing with emergencies. (*Sings mockingly the pre-recorded music she heard earlier*) "Please hold while we put you through" (*Sings the music again.*)

BRENDA. Anna, please.

Silence.

ANNA. What's the point of private security anyway?

BRENDA. What do you mean? Look around. See how efficient these guys are!

ANNA. . . . Yes . . . But you're with Armed Response—right?

BRENDA. Yes.

ANNA. Last night, when you got attacked, you pressed the panic button?

BRENDA. Of course.

ANNA. And they were supposed to get there immediately.

BRENDA. . . . Yes

ANNA. Well, tell me—where were they when your husband got beaten up?

BRENDA. They arrived. Few minutes after those . . . bastards left. (*Pause*) All happened so quickly. Not their fault that they were late. (*Pause*) They told us to upgrade our contract. We didn't.

ANNA. But you've got these high walls, panic buttons, alarm—

BRENDA. But we don't have an electric fence. We didn't take their advice.

ANNA. So you're saying it's your fault.

Pause.

BRENDA. In a way.

ANNA. You're crazy.

BRENDA. Get real Anna, this is Johannesburg. Look what happened to you last night. You could have been killed. (*Pause*) Know what those men did to my husband? Made him keep his legs straight. Said it was the best way to break every bone.

Silence. Inspector enters.

INSPECTOR. Morning ladies. I'm sorry I won't be able to see you today.

ANNA. Inspector—We've been here for ages!

INSPECTOR. I understand. But so have I.

ANNA. That's your job!

INSPECTOR. No need to shout. I've been here since 7 a.m. listening to hundreds of voice-mail messages. Why do people always have to call at night? It'll take me the whole day to get through the rest.

BRENDA. Sorry to bother you, officer. But my husband—

INSPECTOR. What about him?

BRENDA. He's in hospital. Last night they—

INSPECTOR. So he's alive?

BRENDA. Yes, but—

INSPECTOR. Tell him to come see me when he's better.

BRENDA. But I'm here now.

INSPECTOR. Who was attacked, you or him?

BRENDA. . . . He was.

INSPECTOR. Then he has to fill out the form. We only accept personal statements. Now I really must go. (*He turns to leave.*)

ANNA. Wait!

INSPECTOR. What now?

ANNA. I have a personal statement to make.

INSPECTOR. Tomorrow.

ANNA. No, now! *Das darf doch nicht wahr sein!*

INSPECTOR. German?

ANNA. Yes.

INSPECTOR. Come through.

BRENDA. But—

INSPECTOR. Goodbye. My best wishes to your husband. (*He turns and walks to his office. Anna follows him. Brenda pauses, then leaves. Cross-fade to Inspector's office. The both sit at his desk. He has telephone books on his desk and thick black pens.*) Look how much work I have to do. Please be brief.

ANNA. What are you doing with all these phone books?

INSPECTOR. Murdered people must be crossed out.

ANNA. . . . in phone books?

INSPECTOR. Yes. These are my files. Chief wants monthly updates. Phone company needs copies.

ANNA. You are crossing out the names of all the murdered people—in phone books?

INSPECTOR. Someone has to do it. (*Pause*) What's your story?

ANNA (*pause*). I was attacked outside my house last night.

INSPECTOR. Raped?

ANNA. . . . No.

INSPECTOR. Robbed?

ANNA. . . . No.

INSPECTOR. Stabbed or shot?

ANNA. . . . No.

INSPECTOR. Then what are you doing here? Can't you see how busy I am? (*Mutters under his breath*) Foreigners wasting my time . . .

ANNA. I said I was attacked! That's why I'm here. If you call the police, nothing happens. You can leave messages. But no one bothers to come! Brenda left four . . .

INSPECTOR. If you'd give me half a chance, I'd listen to her messages. But here you are, keeping me from doing my work.

ANNA. What kind of work is this?

INSPECTOR. Now I've got a headache. Can you please not scream. (*Silence. Anna sits.*) This job is killing me. Do you know I see a psychiatrist? We talk a lot. Look . . . (*he takes out a few photos*) . . . my kids. Barely get to see them. Spend all my days here. (*Pause*) Did you smell the passage? . . . Everyone pisses there. No one cares. Smell drives me crazy. (*Pause*) Look at me. Do you see a policeman?

ANNA. . . . Yes.

INSPECTOR. Bullshit. And this place—You call this a station? An old computer, fucked up car, three cops on a bullshit salary and a building that smells of piss. (*He deletes more names in the phone book.*)

Silence.

VOICE FROM OFFSTAGE. Inspector—Everything in order?

INSPECTOR. All fine, Moses.

VOICE FROM OFFSTAGE. I'll be outside if you need me.

INSPECTOR. Okay, thanks! (*To Anna*) Good thing we got private security guards to keep us safe.

ANNA. *Ich kann das nicht glauben!*[7] . . . If this was Germany, you'd have to protect your own station. Wouldn't have time to sit here all day. You'd be out helping people. You'd have come out last night to help me!

INSPECTOR. Lady, if this was Germany, I'd have a decent salary. Be driving a Mercedes police car with leather seats, air-con, Global Positioning Satellite system—It'd be a pleasure to come out and help you! As it is, if I get into that kaput car outside, I'd either break down on my way to you or get hijacked. If you really want to feel safe go with a private security company— go with Armed Response.

Silence. Inspector continues deleting names from the phone book.

ANNA. I want to report an assault.

INSPECTOR. I want to be German.

ANNA. What?

INSPECTOR. I want to be a German professor.

ANNA. Excuse me?

INSPECTOR. Professor of Security Studies at Berlin University. (*Silence*) German salary, nice car, no stress. Office full of flowers, smiling perfumed personal assistant, floors freshly waxed—twice a day.

Silence.

ANNA. I said I want to report an assault.

INSPECTOR. And I said I want to go to Germany.

ANNA. What the hell can I do about that? (*Silence. Inspector smiles warmly at her.*) You're asking . . . you expect me to . . . (*Inspector smiles more warmly at her.*) . . . If I get you this . . . job, you'll find the guy who attacked me. (*Inspector smiles even more warmly at her.*) . . . Berlin University . . . I could write to an uncle.

---

7 I can't believe this.

INSPECTOR. Let's get you the form. (*Exits.*)

Anna follows him.

Scene 13

Anna's house. Anna is putting up bars.

ANNA (*voice on tape*). I leave the police station. Walk down the street. Stop outside the old stock exchange. Huge steel-and-glass building glaring at the sun. (*Pause*) I am in the middle of a crowd. I smell everyone's sweat. The smell of bodies trying to survive under the sun. The summer heat of Jo'burg's streets. I need to get out. Where did I park?

I find my car, I have survived. I am safe. Can't believe that I miss not seeing a policeman. Every fourth car belongs to Armed Response. But not a cop in sight. I unlock the gearlock, press the hidden little button waiting for the beep. This disarms the satellite tracking system. I convince myself I am streetwise, but anxiously glance around to see if there are any potential hijackers.

I stop at a busy intersection. A man comes up to my car. What does he want? He has no shoes, baggy khaki shorts, a torn T-shirt. He shows me a crumpled plastic bag. It's filled with his garbage art. Cars made out of coke cans, sprite cans, beer cans crafted in the shape of a petrol tanker. The man says nothing, I don't want to talk to him. I give him some money . . . The cars he makes with his own hands are the only vehicles he will ever own.

Scene 14

The bar. Themba, Zama and Vusi drinking.

VUSI. Why the fuck did you have to break his legs?

THEMBA. We waited for the German girl. She didn't pitch. I was pissed off!

VUSI. You went too far!

THEMBA. We didn't kill him.

VUSI. You don't get it—do you?

THEMBA. Get what?

VUSI. The whole neighborhood is shit scared now.

THEMBA. So?

VUSI. They're our clients. They think we look after them. If we do a little number 1 on them, they call us, we arrive a few minutes late, as usual, they still think we look after them. But, if one of them gets hit so badly, they'll all freak out. Think we're not doing our job and go for some other company! We'll lose the whole street, the neighborhood.

ZAMA. It's all about keeping the balance. Just enough crime is good. Too much hard core is bad for business.

THEMBA. It was just one hit. What's the big deal?

VUSI. The deal is you were supposed to scare them so they would do the upgrade.

THEMBA. That's what I did.

ZAMA. You put him in hospital for a month.

THEMBA. So, I pushed it a bit.

VUSI. Pushed it a bit! He'll be so pissed off now, he'll probably leave Armed Response altogether. Along with the rest.

THEMBA. You worry too much. Anyway, it's your Anna's fault. We should sort her out. But you keep stopping us. How come she never pitched last night? We heard some guy attacked her. But he didn't take anything. She wasn't even touched. Now, isn't that a little strange, Vusi?

VUSI. . . . Anything can happen out there . . .

THEMBA. You're telling us there's some new guy working the streets. Who? How come we don't know about him? This is your fucking territory!—Or maybe you do know him . . . maybe we all do.

ZAMA. What are you trying to say?

THEMBA. Whatever. (*To Vusi*) Call me when you figure out what to do with your . . . Anna. (*Pause*) Word is you're losing your touch. If you don't sort this out—fast, Boss will sort you out. (*Exits.*)

ZAMA. Bastard.

VUSI. What's he up to? What's he telling the Boss? Did he see him?

ZAMA. He's been seeing a lot of him.

VUSI. About what?

ZAMA. He's after your job, man. (*Silence*) You held her up last night, didn't you. (*Pause*) Why?

VUSI. . . . Didn't want her to get hurt.

ZAMA. You're fucking out, man. She's the one causing all the shit.

VUSI. It's not just the girl! I'm *gatvol*[8] of making people paranoid.

ZAMA. Paranoia is our business, and you know it. You're risking everything for this girl. And Themba's waiting for you to fuck up. (*Pause*) If she doesn't take that contract, Boss will have her killed. And you'll lose your job.

VUSI. No, I won't! (*He takes out his cellphone and dials*) Boss! I just wanted to tell you everything's fine . . . Yes! She signed . . . I've got it right here. . . . Zama's with me. I'll bring it to you . . . tomorrow. . . . No, I can't. Car's giving trouble, wheel alignment. I'm at Mike's chop shop now—(*Shouting into space*) Hey, Mike! How long will it be, man? I know it's Sunday! But how long?— (*Into phone*) Looks like it'll take all afternoon. . . . Okay, thanks, Boss. See you tomorrow.

ZAMA. What the fuck have you done?!

VUSI. I . . . I had to buy some time.

ZAMA. Never mind losing your job . . . you're dead, man.

VUSI. I've got tonight, tomorrow morning. I'll go to her now. I know she'll do it. Yes, she'll do it. Where's that paper? Where is it, man? At her place. Left it on her table. Okay, okay, all I have to do is get her to sign it.

ZAMA (*shouts*). You lied to the Boss! Told him it was done. And that I saw it! You're finished, man! (*Exits.*)

Vusi follows.

Scene 15

Anna's house. She is putting up more bars. We hear her doorbell ring.

ANNA. I'm coming! (*Doorbell rings again.*) I said I'm coming! (*Exits.*)

Vusi rushes in, followed by Anna.

VUSI. You're locking your front door now. Good.

ANNA. What the hell are you doing here? Get out!

VUSI. Look I'll be quick.

---

8 South African word, derived from the Afrikaans language; fed-up or irritated.

ANNA. Out!

VUSI. Anna, listen to me—things are getting out of hand.

ANNA. What are you talking about?

VUSI. Where is it? Was on the table. I'm sure it was. Where is it?!

ANNA. Don't shout at me! Get away from there.

VUSI. Where's that paper? What have you done with it? We have to have it!

ANNA. I'm warning you—get out! (*Anna goes to the phone, dials. Vusi nervously rummages through the papers on her table.*) Hello? Is that the police? Hello? Hello? Where? Umzim what? Um-zim-ku-lu Police Station?! Can you please put me through to—hello? Who? Sepati? I know you, we spoke before. You're in Cape Town. Yes I'm fine thank you. No I'm not fine actually. There's a guy here . . . no he's not attacking me but I—what? Yes, that's right—I'm in Jo'burg. . . . Hello? Hello? Sepati? Who? Londiwe? From Gabba what? Gabba-rone Bot-swana?! (*She slams the phone down.*)

VUSI. Found it! You haven't signed?

ANNA. Please, just leave.

VUSI. Anna you must .

ANNA. Don't come near me!

VUSI. YOU DON'T KNOW THE DANGER YOU'RE IN!

ANNA. Get away from me! (*She grabs a metal burglar bar from the floor.*)

He grips her arm.

VUSI. I'm trying to help you! (*She tries to fight him off. Vusi forces the bar out of her hand and holds it. Anna backs away, terrified.*) I'm not . . . going to hurt you. (*Pause, he keeps holding the bar.*) Sign . . . please.

ANNA. You're behind everything.

VUSI. What?

ANNA. That's why you keep coming back—you want to break my legs also?

VUSI. Are you crazy?

ANNA. I know you did it to him.

VUSI. I haven't done anything to anybody! Christ, woman, can't you see what's happening.

ABOVE: *Tsepo Wa Mamatu (Vusi, standing) and Tarryn Lee (Anna, bending).*
BELOW: *Lunga Radebe (Themba), Tarryn Lee (Anna).*
Photograph by Sally Gaule.

ABOVE, FROM LEFT TO RIGHT: *Lunga Radebe (Themba), Jerry Mntonga (Zama), Tsepo Wa Mamatu (Vusi)*.

BELOW, FROM LEFT TO RIGHT: *Tarryn Lee (Anna), Tsepo Wa Mamatu (Vusi)*.

Photograph by Sally Gaule.

ANNA. I can see. Very clearly. If people don't do what you say, you go for them. You break their legs.

VUSI. Anna, listen to me. You're in danger. Not from me . . . Please, just do this one thing, and you'll be fine.

ANNA. And if I don't ? Something will happen to me? What?

VUSI. Just fucking do it! (*He grabs her and forces her to the table.*)

Anna fights back.

ANNA (*screams*). Let go of me! LET GO!

LERATO (*rushing in*). Anna, are you . . . what the hell . . . (*Taking out her gun*) Let go of her! I said, let-her-go! (*Vusi lets go.*) Drop the bar! Drop it! (*Vusi puts the bar down.*) Don't move!

VUSI. I can explain everything

LERATO. Don't come any closer!

VUSI (*stops*). Please . . . let me explain. I have been—

LERATO. Stay there! No! Get out! (*She points the gun, unsure.*)

VUSI. Lady, please, I—

LERATO. Get out NOW! (*She cocks the gun . . .*)

VUSI (*backs towards the door*). Look . . . I'm sorry . . . I'll leave . . . I'm going . . . see . . . the paper . . . Anna, please . . . sign it. I'll . . . I'll come for it tomorrow. Ten o'clock! (*Exits.*)

They look at each other. Lerato holds Anna in her arms. Cross-fade to next scene.

Scene 16

The bar. Zama is having a drink. Vusi enters.

VUSI. I really need your help, man.

ZAMA. How could you do that to me? How could you tell the Boss WE had the contract? Hey?

VUSI. Zama, I'm sorry. I didn't know what to say.

ZAMA. Now, I'm in shit up to my neck!

VUSI. I messed up, but I'll sort this out. I promise.

ZAMA. You put the Boss on my back! (*Silence*) Never seen you like this before. Running around like a headless chicken. All for a girl.

VUSI. . . . She's different.

ZAMA. She's a pain in the neck.

VUSI. . . . Sticks to her guns . . .

ZAMA. She's pigheaded!

VUSI. She's not . . . a coward.

Silence.

ZAMA. The principal is.

VUSI. What?

ZAMA. A coward. Those kids are still at it. Take the lunch boxes from the Grade Ones. Now he's hiring a shrink for them. All parents have to pay 50 rands extra per term!

VUSI. Crazy. (*Silence*) Where's Themba?

Silence.

ZAMA. We had no choice—I'm sorry.

VUSI. What do you mean?

ZAMA. Themba's solving your problem.

VUSI. What?

ZAMA. He's gone to her house. He'll deal with her.

VUSI. You just let him go there?

ZAMA. We're trying to help you, man.

VUSI. Shit! Zama, I trusted you!

ZAMA. It's the only way out. You're not yourself, Vusi. Someone had to act.

VUSI. He'll kill her!

ZAMA. No, he won't. He'll just persuade her to change her mind.

VUSI. Persuade her?

ZAMA. He'll make sure.

VUSI. Zama, you know how Themba works! Shit, I have to get there now!

ZAMA. Vusi! Wait!

Vusi exits.

Scene 17

Cross fade back to Anna and Lerato in Anna's house.

LERATO. You sure you don't want me to stay?

ANNA. No, I'm fine.

LERATO. I'll sleep over tonight.

ANNA. Thanks, but you really don't have to.

LERATO. . . . Will you be okay?

ANNA. Yes. It's late. You need to get back.

LERATO. You look exhausted.

ANNA. I'm wasted.

LERATO. Can I make you some coffee before I go?

ANNA. No, thank you.

> *Pause.*

LERATO. If you need anything, remember I'm right next door.

ANNA. Okay.

> *Lerato turns to go, then stops and looks at Anna.*

LERATO. Don't forget to lock. (*Exits.*)

> *Anna gets up to lock the door, but then decides to have a drink first. She takes out a bottle of whiskey and drinks. She gets some food from the fridge, then remembers the contract. She goes to find it among her papers on the table. She thinks about signing it. Exhausted, she falls asleep on the couch.*

> *Themba enters through the unlocked door. He stops, looks at the sleeping Anna. He hovers at the light switch, turns the light off. He goes to get some blue cheese and juice from the fridge and leaves the fridge door open. A gleam of light emanates from the fridge. He eats and drinks. Then he puts his balaclava on. He carefully picks up the metal burglar bar from the floor and deliberately tosses it to the other side of the room. Anna wakes up, startled. She stares at where the sound came from.*

ANNA. Who's there? (*Themba stands behind Anna and whistles the "Dead Dog Blues". She spins around to face him. We only see his silhouette in the light from the fridge.*) What do you want? (*She backs away from him. He whistles the tune.*) Vusi? (*Silence.*) I know it's you, Vusi! (*He approaches slowly.*) I'm not scared of you! (*He pulls out a gun, holds it to her neck. Terrified, she arches her neck back. With his free hand he slowly caresses her hair and mouth. He parts her lips, puts his finger on her lips, then licks his finger. He motions with his gun for her to lie on the couch. Anna backs toward the couch. She half falls onto it. He whistles again, unbuckles his belt, unzips his pants. He stops whistling, carefully puts his gun on the table. He slowly forces her down onto the couch and lies on top of her. Anna screams. He puts his hand over her mouth. Silence. Vusi is on the street and cocks his gun Themba freezes, listens hard. Vusi has disappeared. We hear the sound of a brick smashing a window. Themba jumps up, swears and runs out. He forgets his gun on the table. Anna moves to the "window" on the edge of the platform, shouts—)* Who's there? *(Pause)* Lerato?

Silence. Anna goes back inside. She leans against the side of the fridge and slowly slides down into a crouching position.

Scene 18

Anna's house. She gets up, picks up the phone. She dials.

ANNA. Hello! Please put me through to Greenside Police Station. Thank you
. . . Inspector? . . . I can't believe I got you! Thank God . . . Sorry, I know
it's late. . . . I . . . I nearly got raped . . . now . . . he ran off . . . sound of a
gun . . . from outside . . . No, but I know who it was . . . yes, I'm sure. It's
that guy from Armed Response . . . I don't know his last name . . . Vusi.
Ever since I got here he's been trying to force me to join their company
. . . No, I haven't joined. But he said he'd be back tomorrow . . . at 10.
Please, you have to come! . . . Now! My door is broken! . . . What if he comes
back? . . . Can't you get another car? . . . *Arschloch!* Fuck it, I'll find a way
. . . But you will come . . . tomorrow . . . Thank you. *(She puts the phone down,
picks up the gun that Themba has left on the table. Music comes up. Silhouetted,
Anna finishes putting up the bars.)*

Anna's house, on the platform, now looks like a cage.

Scene 19

Next morning. Vusi is waiting in the street outside Anna's house. Zama enters.

VUSI. Where you been man?

ZAMA. You said 10 o'clock.

VUSI. I said quarter-to!

ZAMA (*calming him down*). Okay, okay . . . I'm here now. You were really freaking on the phone last night.

VUSI. Sorry I called you so late.

ZAMA. It's okay. What happened with Themba and the girl?

VUSI. Don't know. I got here, was going to shoot. But I threw a brick through the window to scare him. He ran off.

ZAMA. Was she okay?

VUSI. I think so.

ZAMA. I'm sure Themba did the job. She'll do what we want. And if she doesn't I'll finish her off. (*Pause*) We get rid of this hassle—next client in that house takes out a contract. Then we can all get on with our lives.

Silence.

VUSI. When I come out—if you see me walking that way, wait five minutes before you go in.

Vusi and Zama leave in different directions.

Scene 20

Anna's house, brightly lit. It's now fully caged in. Bars surround the whole platform. Vusi rings the doorbell and she is startled.

ANNA. Who's there?

Pause. Anna grabs the gun.

VUSI. Anna, it's me, Vusi. (*Silence. She gets up, backs away from the door, petrified.*) Anna, please open! (*Silence. Vusi rings the bell again.*) I have to talk to you. (*Silence*) Let me in! (*Silence. Vusi breaks the door offstage and enters.*)

Anna is holding the gun. He walks toward her, holding his arms half up.

ANNA. Stop!

VUSI. Anna, please . . .

ANNA. Don't come any closer!

VUSI. Put the gun down.

ANNA. Get over there!

VUSI. I'm not going hurt you! We have to talk.

ANNA. Move! (*Vusi moves to the side.*) I know what you've been doing.

VUSI. We don't have time for this.

ANNA. You sent those guys to scare me. They held a lighter in my face. You smashed my window. You had me blindfolded . . . on my knees. . . . You broke my neighbor's legs . . . nearly raped me last night. Had your dirty hands all over me! . . . Now you break in here! Get out! Out!

Silence.

VUSI. Anna, you're wrong.

ANNA. Don't come near me.

VUSI. Anna.

ANNA. Shut up!

VUSI. Listen to me for once!

ANNA. GET OUT!

VUSI. You've got it all wrong. I never touched you. Last night . . . the guy was about to rape you . . . then you heard a gun, had a brick through the window . . . it was me.

Pause.

ANNA. I don't believe you.

VUSI. So how do I know about it? (*Pause*) I was outside. Over there.

ANNA. You were in here.

VUSI. Anna, it wasn't me. It was Themba. (*Pause*) That's how the Company works. If you don't make a deal with them, they do a hit on you. Scare you. No one can stop them. They're connected everywhere.

Pause.

ANNA. . . . What . . . no . . . that was you . . . I heard the whistling . . .

VUSI. It was a hit-man from Armed Response.

ANNA. . . . This . . . can't be true . . .

VUSI. That night you were attacked in the street . . . it was me . . . you know why? . . . He was waiting for you. Here, in your house. I had to keep you outside, away from him.

Silence.

ANNA. You blindfolded me?

VUSI. I couldn't let you see me.

Pause.

ANNA. You forced me on my knees . . .

VUSI. I had to. So that Themba couldn't see you. I kept you hidden behind those bricks. Didn't hurt you, did I? . . . (*Pause*) The other time, when you were sitting outside on your own . . . there was a gunshot.

ANNA. I remember.

VUSI. . . . Some guy was about to mug you. I dragged him away. Just in time.

ANNA. You shot him?

VUSI. Anna . . .

ANNA. I don't believe this.

Pause.

VUSI. I've been trying to keep you from getting hurt . . . or worse.

ANNA. . . . Why . . .

VUSI. Why couldn't you just sign with the Company? Why did you have to fuck it up? And now you got the whole neighborhood scared. They all want to cancel.

Pause.

ANNA. Why did you do it? (*She lowers the gun. Silence*) Why didn't you tell me?

Themba enters.

THEMBA. You're a dirty piece of work, man.

VUSI. Themba! What you doing here?

THEMBA. Got a call. You know how it is these days—Can't trust anyone, Vusi.

VUSI. Where's Zama?

THEMBA. Never mind. Where's your sense of loyalty?

VUSI. What . . . what have you heard?

THEMBA. Everything. All the stories you told your German girlfriend. Give me my gun, baby. (*He moves towards Anna.*)

She grabs the gun on the table.

ANNA. Don't move!

THEMBA. Take it easy. We were getting so close last night. (*He licks his finger*) I can still taste you.

VUSI. Themba! Back off!

THEMBA. Shut up, Vusi. You're history. She's mine now. We'll have a good time. (*He moves closer to Anna.*)

VUSI. I said BACK OFF!

THEMBA. You fucked this up, brother. I'm in charge now. You told her everything. I'll put a bullet in your brain, Judas.

VUSI. You wouldn't dare!

THEMBA. Watch me.

ANNA. If you come any closer, I'll shoot!

THEMBA. Give me the gun. Come on!—(*Softly*) Give it to Uncle Themba.

ANNA. I'm warning you!

He reaches Anna, gently puts his hand over the muzzle and slowly pulls the gun towards him. Anna doesn't let go but tries to jerk it back. A shot goes off. Themba falls. Silence. Vusi goes to the body. Silence.

VUSI. He's dead. (*Pause*) You had no choice.

ANNA. . . . It just went off . . .

Silence.

VUSI. He was going to rape you. (*Silence*) Don't worry. No one needs to know.

ANNA. The police . . .

VUSI. What about them?

ANNA. They're coming.

VUSI. What?

ANNA. I called them last night . . . to be here at 10.

VUSI. Why did you call them?

ANNA. . . . I'll go to jail.

VUSI. Why did you call the cops?

Silence.

ABOVE, FROM LEFT TO RIGHT: *Tsepo Wa Mamatu (Vusi), Lunga Radebe (Themba), Tarryn Lee (Anna)*.

BELOW, FROM LEFT TO RIGHT: *Tarryn Lee (Anna) and Tsepo Wa Mamatu (Vusi)*.

Photograph by Sally Gaule.

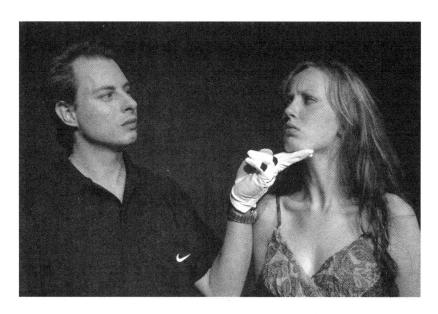

ABOVE, FROM LEFT TO RIGHT: *Brian Webber* (Boss), *Tarryn Lee* (Anna).
BELOW, FROM LEFT TO RIGHT: *Brian Webber* (Boss), *Tsepo Wa Mamatu* (Vusi).
Photograph by Sally Gaule.

ANNA. You . . . I thought it was you. All of it. You were coming at 10. I wanted them to be here . . . arrest you. Now they'll take me.

VUSI. Self-defence. I'll tell them. (*The Boss enters. He looks at Anna. Notices the gun in her hand and the body on the floor.*) Boss!

BOSS. So you're Anna. Pleased to meet you. I'm Paul. Managing Director of Armed Response. (*Pause*) What happened here?

ANNA. . . . . You're not the police?

BOSS (*smiles*). Police are for traffic fines. So, I hear you signed?

VUSI. We . . . were just talking about it.

BOSS. Seems there was some disagreement.

VUSI. I can explain everything, Boss.

BOSS. Anna, do you have mango juice?

ANNA. . . . . Yes. (*Puts the gun down, goes to the fridge to get the juice.*)

BOSS. Pure, not concentrated?

ANNA. . . . . Yes.

BOSS. Wonderful. Lots of ice, please. Thank you . . . (*Looking through the burglar bars*) Nice view. Beautiful jacarandas outside. (*Puts his arm around Vusi*) Don't you think, Vusi?

VUSI. Yes, Boss.

BOSS (*tightening the grip on Vusi*). What the fuck happened to Themba? What's going on here?

VUSI. It was an accident. Gun went off.

BOSS. You bullshitting me?

VUSI. Boss, I swear, it's the truth!

Anna returns with the juice, Boss lets go of Vusi.

BOSS. Thank you. Vusi, we'll discuss this later. (*Sits down comfortably with his juice*) So, Anna. You tell me what happened here.

VUSI. . . . . He tried to rape her.

BOSS. I'm sorry about that.

VUSI. It was self-defence.

BOSS (*to Anna*). So you shot him.

ANNA. . . . Yes.

BOSS (*sips some juice*). What an unpleasant way to start the day. Let's get to the good news now. Vusi, would you be so kind as to pass me the contract.

Vusi picks it up from the table and hands it to the Boss.

BOSS. It's not signed. Lucky I have my pen with me. Here we are. (*Hands Anna the pen and paper.*)

Silence. Anna looks at Vusi, looks at Boss, doesn't take the paper.

BOSS. I see. Vusi, you told me it was done.

VUSI. . . . I was going to—

BOSS (*softly*). I can't have people lying to me.

VUSI. I can explain—

BOSS. Let me explain to you—one lie breaks all trust. You and I will have to part ways. Problem is I can't fire you. You could tell everyone about our business strategy. Anna, would you please excuse us.

ANNA. Leave him alone! I'll tell the police.

BOSS. I wouldn't do that if I were you. You just shot someone. You were holding the gun when I came in.

VUSI. I'm telling you—

BOSS. You're on your way out, Vusi. Say goodbye to your friend.

ANNA. He told me!

BOSS. Told you what?

ANNA. About your . . . strategy. I know everything. You'll have to shut us both up . . . only way to keep it quiet. But then you're stuck with three corpses. Here, in one house in one day! Whole street will know about it, the neighborhood. You'll have hundreds of cancellations! Your balance, remember your balance! (*Pause*) I'll sign! Let him go and I'll sign.

VUSI. Anna, don't!

Anna takes the contract and quickly signs.

BOSS. This might turn out to be a pleasant day after all. Problem is, he broke the rules. Honesty, confidentiality. He could have . . . an accident. Any day. Bad wheel alignment.

ANNA. If anything happens to him, I'll make sure everyone knows about you.

BOSS. Oh no, you won't. Then I'll make sure everyone knows what you did to Themba. (*Pause*) You shot him. Who do you think the police will believe? (*Silence. Takes out his phone, smiles. He dials, speaks into phone*) They're ready. (*Switches the phone off. Inspector enters.*) Good to see you, Thabo.

INSPECTOR. You too, Paul.

ANNA. Inspector?

INSPECTOR. The German girl! Enjoying your visit?

BOSS. We have a problem.

INSPECTOR (*looking at the body*). I can see.

BOSS. The guys had an argument. This one got carried away, shot his colleague.

Silence. Inspector advances on Vusi. He is terrified. Inspector grabs him, handcuffs him.

VUSI. Anna! (*Pause, softly*) Please . . .

Inspector looks at Anna. She glances at him and the Boss, then looks down. Silence. Vusi is led out by the Inspector. Pause.

BOSS. We'll put the Company logo outside your house. Anna, I throw in a 50 percent discount for you. I'll get an artist in. The logo will have taste and gravitas. (*He shakes Anna's hands*) Welcome to Johannesburg.

Boss exits. Anna sits down, stunned. Advert from Scene 1 begins. It is projected onto the back wall behind the bars. It ends with the Armed Response logo (with taste and gravitas) designed especially for Anna. Lights slowly fade. Blackout.

End of Play

NOTES ON CONTRIBUTORS

MPUMELELO PAUL GROOTBOOM has been the recipient of the National Standard Bank Young Artist Award for Theater (2005) and the Naledi Theatre Award for *Relativity* (2005). His work has toured Australia, the U.K., and numerous European cities. He was resident writer with the North West Arts Council in 1997, and has been Development Officer of the South African State Theatre since 2002. His television writing includes *Isidingo*, *Soul City*, and *Healside* (which he also directed). He has written and directed numerous plays including *Relativity: Township Stories* (with Presley Chweneyagae) (2004), *Telling Stories* (2007), and *Interracial* (with Aubrey Sekhabi) (2007).

PRESLEY CHWENEYAGAE is a very well-known South African actor and writer. He is best known for his starring performance in the Oscar winning film *Tsotsi* (2005).

MARTIN KOBOEKAE's—playwright, journalist, novelist, theatre director—first play *Short Hair, Flat Nose* caused a sensation in 1992. His plays *Cats and Dogs*, *The Dream*, *Things Men Do*, have all won South African Windybrow/FNB Vita Awards in different categories. Koboekae's other plays include *Location 1973*, *Wicked Confessions*, *Horroscope*, *Nasty Moments*, *Third Coming*, *Mr. Flat Nose*, and *BIKO: Where the Soul Resides* (2008 Grahamstown National Arts Festival). Author of the acclaimed novel *Taung Wells* (2004), he is Co-director, National Stop Crime Drama Festival; Chairperson, Utlwanang Theatre; Secretary, United Theatre Practitioners—committed to community theater initiatives. His next novel, *The Cleanser*, will be published soon.

XOLI NORMAN has lectured at Wits University, Johannesburg (2001–03) and worked for the Market Theatre Laboratory (1989–2000). He has been commissioned by the Namibian National Theatre to conduct community theater-development training workshops for the Arts and Culture government officials (2002). He has been guest lecturer at London (Goldsmiths) and Bristol Universities (2001) and won the Graham Lindop Young Artists Award (2001) and the Olive Shreiner Theatre Award for *Hallelujah!* (2002). Co-creator of large installations as well as composer and actor for performances for the Prague Quadrennial (2003), Norman has also been Associate Director on the television program "Soul City" (2002) and Co-director for the television series "Riemvasmaak" (2007).

LARA FOOT NEWTON is a director and writer whose work has been acclaimed nationally and internationally. Committed to developing South African theater, she has directed over 34 productions: 23 of new South African works, including staging Zakes Mda's novel, *Ways of Dying* (2000) and *Tshepang* (2003), her devastating portrayal of the South African phenomenon of infant rape that won Best New Play Award (2003; published 2004). Her work has toured internationally, and she has taught acting and directing. In 2004, she won the prestigious *Rolex* Mentor and Protégé Arts Award and was protégé to Sir Peter Hall. Her plays—*Reach* and *Karoo Moose* (2007)—have won nine *Fleur du Cap* nominations. She is a Sundance Fellow and is working on the film adaptation of *Tshepang*. She is published by Oberon Books, Wits Press, and has a Masters degree from the University of Cape Town.

DAVID PEIMER has written and directed numerous plays including *Smell*, *Last Revolt*, *Scavenger's Dream*, and *Serpent's Mate*. A former Fulbright Scholar (Columbia University), he has presented work at Oxford, London, Columbia, Toronto, Bristol, N.Y.U. (Prague) Universities, and others, and directed his plays in Johannesburg, London, Bristol (U.K.), Prague, Cape Town. President Havel invited him to stage theater in Prague and he created a major art installation with performances for the Prague Quadrennial (2003). Plays directed include those by Shakespeare, Aristophanes, Beckett, Buchner, Heiner Muller, and Fassbinder. Awards include the George Soros Fellowship, Goethe Institute Fellowship, and South African National Amstel Playwriting Awards. He has taught at Wits University (Johannesburg) and at N.Y.U. (Prague).